SILENCES AND NONSENSES

Collected Poetry, Doggerel and Whimsy

Adrian Plass

The world is very big and round
and in it many things are found
Eg.
A Bee

This book is for Bridget, who has been my wife for nearly forty years and my friend for even longer. Her consistent care and support are part of everything that I write and say and do. She reads poetry (including mine) more beautifully than anyone else I know. Bridget has done nearly all of the work involved in getting this collection together, and I am sincerely grateful. I dedicate it to her with all my love.

FOREWORD

I did something rather dreadful once. It happened during my second visit to a monthly poetry group meeting at the college where I was training to be an English teacher. I had written only a handful of poems at that time, but lodged inside my failing soul was a small, secret hope that I might be a lyrical genius. Cowardly as ever, I decided not to take any examples of my work with me to the first meeting in case it turned out that I wasn't.

About fifteen people turned up for that first session. We sat around a big table made up of lots of little tables, every person except me armed with notebooks or sheets of paper. After twenty minutes or so I was seriously glad I hadn't brought my stuff. It all seemed so intense and obscure. I had problems understanding nearly every line of every poem I heard. Latin tags and bits of Greek and German abounded, and people seemed so deeply, almost tearfully moved by the sound of their own voices performing their own work. It was just a mist. I felt stupid.

It's amazing how quickly you learn, though, isn't it? I soon caught on to the fact that there were three ways of reacting to each offering.

Nodding was one response. I could do that. I developed a parsimoniously slight but solemn inclination of the head, designed to indicate that, having brought my vast literary insight to bear on the poem in question, I was pleased to offer gracious but restrained approval. I became quite good at that.

The second response, 'Mmmmm!' was a judicious murmur of appreciation voiced in interesting variations on two, three, or even four notes. I knew I would have to practise that one before next time.

The third option was to lean decisively backwards or forwards in your chair and say, with the air of one who is fascinated by his own rarefied artistic and intellectual curiosity, 'I think I'd like to hear that again.'

As the time for my second visit drew near I wondered if there was a way to test whether this intimidating group was for real. I decided to read them something that was not actually a poem and see what they made of it. I should have told them the whole truth really, shouldn't I? I didn't. This is what I read. Vaguely feeling that I ought at least to offer them a clue, I called it 'Our Times'.

Like the merchandise of wells, the wise men state
Chemical can put up the speed
In part grassland, in all the fold
Swirling ooze contains exotic bed of beastly fossil
There's a sign chlorine is included in nature terminology
At once correct the tiny slant
Literary corporal garlanded in Ireland
Luck begins to change for a literary lady
Wine drunk to noisy Elsinore accompaniment
Beetles learning to ride horses
A plain sort of oyster

This very moving piece was received in different ways by the rest of the group – well, three actually.

They nodded.

They murmured, 'Mmmmm!'

They said, 'I think I'd like to hear that again.'

My subsequent revelation that the 'poem' I had just read was actually the last ten *across* clues in the Times crossword did not go down at all well, but from that day onward I stopped being quite so silly and snobbish about poets and poetry.

All this defensive drivel is a prelude to saying that, although I am not and never will be a great poet, I have immensely enjoyed using a wide variety of poetic forms to express and preserve feelings and events that have been important to me in the course of the last twenty-five years. To have them all, good, not so good, simple, complicated, light-hearted, funny, serious, sensible and silly, collected into one volume is more exciting than I can say. The book is divided into five chronological periods of five years each, with a brief comment at the beginning of each section.

I am so happy to share my Poetry, Doggerel and Whimsy with readers of this book. Enjoy it. Use it. It's for you.

Silences and Nonsenses

1985-1990

HALL OF MIRRORS

What a strange period of my life this was. There is a part of my cowardly soul that groans inwardly every time I have to write or speak or think about clambering up from the depths of the stress illness that changed so many things in 1984. It was all so dismal and dank for a while, and other people suffered as a result of my emotional splurge. On the other hand I experienced a definite if somewhat indiscriminate outburst of creativity that led to a speaking and writing career that took me completely by surprise. One striking revelation was the fact that identity can be found through expression.

The first two poems in this section, *Hall of Mirrors* and *When I was a Small Boy*, reflect the problems I had always found in working out who I was (I grew up in the sixties, remember, so we were always tackling silly questions like that), and *The Preacher* and *Poison Pools* are so filled with the pain of deconstruction that I can hardly read them now. Putting stuff, feelings, whatever, down on paper was like repacking a rucksack so that it becomes manageable. I was a little more in charge of myself, and I began to believe that I might exist and have a shape.

The rest of the pieces from these years are laced with hope and nervous excitement as life, seriously revised faith and my new occupation began to offer undreamed of possibilities. *Shades of Blue* and *Hallelujah in the Back of my Mind* were about the nearest I could get to spelling out this newly discovered optimism. Miserable beggar!

1985–1990

HALL OF MIRRORS

Stranded in the hall of mirrors
I must struggle to avoid
Images that cannot show me
Something long ago destroyed

In the darkness, in the distance
In a corner of my mind
Stands a puzzled child in silence
Lonely, lost and far behind

In imagination only
In my single mirror see
Clear and calm, the one reflection
Of the person that is me

WHEN I WAS A SMALL BOY

When I was a small boy in a small school,
With endless legs
And ears that widely proclaimed a head full of
    emergencies,
When I clung by bleeding fingertips
To thirty-three plus nine,
And cognitive dissonance was just a hard sum,
There were only two crimes.
The first was shouting in the corridors,
The second was to be a fool,
And when the bell,
The blessed bell,
Let me fling my body home,
I thought I might, at least, one day, aspire to rule in hell,
But now, I never hear the bell,
And part of me
Will always be
A fool
Screaming, in some sacred corridor.

GROWBAG WORLD

Upon this giant growbag world
I planted seeds of light
And dreamed a glowing harvest
That would penetrate the night
But as I toiled upon my knees,
They ringed me round with gloom,
Their pockets full of pallid hands,
Their voices full of doom.

'We tell the truth, the truth is dark,
There is no light to save,
Your seeds will never break the earth,
Your garden is a grave.'
And yet I work, I work, I work,
And now my seeds have grown,
I touch the cold and lightless leaves,
And love them as my own.

And will there come a morning soon,
When flowers from the shade,
Will bloom and break, and float, and light
The world that you have made?
How hard, how hard, to paint a dream,
For eyes that cannot shine,
For eyes too dulled by twilight skies,
To see the dawn in mine.

GATWICK AIRPORT

Sad, robotic, angel voices
Softly, sweetly speaking
To a thousand restless souls
Of gateways and departures
To a hundred different lands,
That may flow with milk and honey
Or lay heavy on the spirit
Like the old Egyptian sands.

SHELL

Saw a shell
Rich with mother-of-pearl
Waited
So long
To see the creature that needed such delicate protection
Realised
So late
The creature was long gone
Soaked with sea
Drifting in heaven or hell
But certainly
Not minding

THE PREACHER

The preacher stands, his people's rock,
And prays mid walls of stone,
Oh, let my congregation's doubts
Be greater than my own.

I shall not look at Mrs Cook,
For her salvation's won,
But I shall speak to Rosie Cheek,
The whore of Babylon.

For Rosie will not humble me,
Her sins are rich and red,
And seven devils throng her soul,
So Mrs Cook has said.

Oh, Rosie, do not fail me now,
I need you for a while,
I do not ask that you repent,
If you will only smile.

My curate will not smile at me,
I fear he is devout,
I fear he fears I fear that he
Will shortly find me out.

He is a strong yet humble man,
His words are firm but meek,
He bores me to the depths of hell,
God bless you, Rosie Cheek.

I try to love them all, O Lord,
And preach your holy book,
But faith that can move mountains
Would stop short at Mrs Cook.

The preacher sits. Do angels sing?
Have they now what they seek,
Safe in the arms of endless love,
The soul of Rosie Cheek?

For in the lamplit study now,
The coals are burning low,
As cold salvation freezes fast,
The living waters flow.

O Lord, would she have kept her smile
If she had come to me,
And notwithstanding Mrs Cook,
Be closer now to thee?

STRESS

I've just been up the doctor's.
   I said, 'Help me, Doctor Brown,'
But he said, 'You've got some tablets!'
    and he had this awful frown,
So I said, 'I've struggled up here
   from the other side of town,
Because the Downers break me up
    and then the Uppers get me down.'
    I'm in a mess,
    It causes stress,
    I've tried my best to rest without success,
    I'm holding it together less and less:
    I suffer stress.

Sometimes when I'm feeling very peaceful in my car,
I hear some little clickings and I know I won't get far
Before the clickings turn to clunkings,
    and you know what clunkings are!
And the garage man will take a look,
    and frown and say, 'Aha!
    Your car's a mess!'
    It causes stress,
    I've tried my best to rest without success,
    I'm holding it together less and less:
    I suffer stress.

Papers tell you food is bad, avoid the butcher's meat,
The nasty fatty stuff will clog, and knock you off your feet.
Everything is fatal, from meringues to shredded wheat,
If it wasn't for starvation, I wouldn't dare to eat.
    So food's a mess,
    It causes stress,
    I've tried my best to rest without success,
    I'm holding it together less and less:
    I suffer stress.

The world is full of terrorists who say they've been abused,
They're all against each other, and they're all a bit confused,
'Cause they murder little people,
    and they say when they're accused,
Ah, but if your motivation's right, you have to be excused.'
    It's just a mess,
    It causes stress,
    I've tried my best to rest without success,
    I'm holding it together less and less:
    I suffer stress.

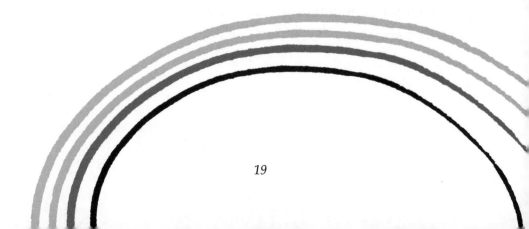

There's weapons pointing east and west,
    they'll soon be flying past,
And I can't sleep for thinking that the end's
    approaching fast,
Every nerve is strained as I await the nuclear blast,
Still – the night they drop the bomb,
    I s'pose I'll get some sleep at last,
    But what a mess,
    It causes stress,
    I've tried my best to rest without success,
    I'm holding it together less and less:
    I suffer stress.

I need a friend to talk to, but they're few and far between,
I ring them up and ask them,
    but they don't seem very keen,
I'm just as sane as they are, and I never make a scene,
They say I'm too neurotic, but I don't know what they mean!
    Oh, what a mess!
    It causes stress,
    I've tried my best to rest without success,
    I'm holding it together less and less
    I suffer stress.

AWAY IN A GUTTER

Away in a gutter,
No food and no bed,
The little Lord Jesus
Hangs down his sweet head.

The stars in the bright sky
Look down and they say,
'The little Lord Jesus
Is wasting away.'

We love you Lord Jesus,
We hope you survive.
We'll see you tomorrow
If you're still alive.

You won't live for long now
With no tender care.
You're best off in heaven,
We'll see you up there

The darkness is lifting
The baby awakes,
But little Lord Jesus,
No movement he makes.

No flesh on his body,
No light in his eye,
The little Lord Jesus
Is going to die.

A FATHER KNOWS NO SADNESS

A father knows no sadness,
No deeper-searching pain,
Than children who have taken,
But will not give again.
What profit from his loving,
If love is never shared,
What insult to his giving,
If nothing can be spared?

They wait for our remembrance,
The ones who live in need,
The ones our father trusts us
To shelter and to feed.
And if you truly love him,
Then they are precious too,
And if they are a burden,
That burden is for you.

THE DREAM OF BEING SPECIAL

And in the summer sunshine
  you believed the things they told you
For it's part of being little
And the trust is right inside you
Like a ball of summer sunshine
In the middle of your body
And you think that it will never fade away
But as the days go flying
You are troubled by the shadows
In the hearts and hands and faces
Of the people you had trusted
When they promised you the sunshine
For you hear the winter now in what they say
And the dream of being special floats away,
And the whole damn thing looks so grey.

And how you'd love to picture the perfection of your lover
Who would be so strong and gentle
That his love would touch your spirit
Through your mind and heart and body
And his tenderness would promise
That the joy of every day would be the same
Then one day you feel frightened
When a man who seemed to like you
Puts his hands upon your shoulders
And he pulls you in towards him
And he holds you far too tightly

And he wants to know your age but not your name
And the dream of being special floats away,
And the whole damn thing looks so grey.

There's a friend you meet on Fridays,
    he's the one who really knows you
And you tell him you're not suited
To the job that you've been doing
But you drink and say don't worry
For I'm planning something different
And I've just about decided on a plan
And won't it be electric when I start my great adventure
And the talent I've been hiding
Has a chance to be discovered
Then you see your friend is smiling
As he smiles every Friday at your dream
And the dream of being special fades away,
And the whole damn thing looks so grey.

And parties they're just places
    where you lean against the doorway
Of the kitchen talking nonsense
To a girl with perfect manners
But you see her eyes are glazing
And you know she's only waiting
For the slightest little chance to get away
So then you fill your glass up
As you nurse your tired passion

And remember all the failures
And you wish to God you hadn't
Overfed your fat opinions
With the food your heart was needing every day
And the dream of being special floats away,
And the whole damn thing looks so grey.

And good old Eamonn Andrews
   would come smiling round the corner
With a big red book and people
Who would say we always loved you
And you'd wonder why the hell they
Never told you when you needed
All the love that they could offer – what a shame
But it really doesn't matter
As it's just another way
To lose the game that you are playing
For in letters that are golden
On that big red book he'd show you
There is someone else's name
And the dream of being special floats away,
And the whole damn thing looks so grey.

POISON POOLS

Who made these poison pools
In desert lands
So sweet and cool?
A welcome lie
The chance to die with water on my lips
I've seen how others try to die unpoisoned in the sun
I do not think that I can do as they have done

WHEN DOES THE JOY START?

The light I have is slowly fading
There's no sign of a change;
Tell me why is this darkness
So sweet and so strange?
Did I think you were joking?
Did I think you were mad
When you told me to follow
The good and the bad?

When does the joy start?
When do the clouds part?
When does the dawn break?
When does the earth shake?
When does the choir sing?
When do the bells ring?
When will I rise with him?

My friends all say I should be leaving,
It may be true that I'm slow,
If you know me like they do
Do you still want to know?
If I knew where to head for,
I would certainly go;
I need someone to tell me,
And you seem to know.

When does the joy start?
When do the clouds part?
When does the dawn break?
When does the earth shake?
When does the choir sing?
When do the bells ring?
When will I rise with him?

I shall not move until you bless me,
I will stand by the door,
In your moment of leaving
You will see me I'm sure.
All I need is a moment,
All I ask is a smile,
Just to know that you love me,
That'll do for a while.

That's when the joy starts,
That's when the dawn breaks,
That's when the earth shakes,
That's when the choir sings,
That's when the bells ring,
That's when I'll rise with him.

That's when you'll see me,
That's when my star falls,
That's when my God calls,
Calls out to my heart,
That's when the joy starts,
That's when I'll rise with him

I DIDN'T HAVE TO SEE YOU

I didn't have to see you
In the night-time, there by the side of me.
I knew it had to be you,
Knew you loved the child inside of me.
You smiled in the darkness,
It seemed to blind and burn,
But when my eyes were opened,
I smiled in return, for you were there.

I didn't have to hear you
In the silence you were a part of me,
I knew that I was near you,
Knew your love was deep in the heart of me,
I knew that you were saying,
Our happiness has grown,
For prayer is only friendship,
You never were alone, for I was there.

I didn't have to hold you,
I was trusting, knowing your care for me,
The secrets I had told you,
Knowing you would always be there for me,
So let the darkness gather,
And let the silence roll,
The love that made you suffer,
Is glowing in my soul, and you are there.

WINTER WALK

I wish I was my son again,
The first in all the world to know
The cornflake crunch of frosted grass
Beside the polar paving stones,
Beneath the drip of liquid light
From watercolour winter suns.

SHADES OF BLUE

Does winter end in seaside towns
When councils paint anew
The railings on the promenade
In hopeful shades of blue?

And if the tide loved Brighton beach
Would God come down and say
With gentle hands upon the surf
'You need not turn today?'

Will massive Church of England bells
Have faith enough to ring
And overcome their weariness
When they believe in spring?

Are there machines for measuring
The power of my prayers
And anyway, and anyway,
And anyway, who cares?

I think you care, but gently,
I think, because you do,
The colour of my sadness
Is a hopeful shade of blue.

I WATCH

I watch
Frightened
Helpless
But secretly willing
As my foot rises, moving forward with my weight,
And I realise
That at last
I am going to walk

WHEN I BECAME A CHRISTIAN

When I became a Christian I said, Lord, now fill me in,
Tell me what I'll suffer in this world of shame and sin.
He said, Your body may be killed, and left to rot and stink,
Do you still want to follow me? I said, Amen – I think.
I think Amen, Amen I think, I think I say Amen,
I'm not completely sure,
    can you just run through that again?
You say my body may be killed and left to rot and stink,
Well, yes, that sounds terrific, Lord, I say Amen – I think.

But, Lord, there must be other ways to follow you, I said,
I really would prefer to end up dying in my bed.
Well, yes, he said, you could put up with sneers and scorn
    and spit,
Do you still want to follow me? I said, Amen! – a bit.
A bit Amen, Amen a bit, a bit I say Amen,
I'm not entirely sure, can we just run through that again?
You say I could put up with sneers and also scorn and spit,
Well, yes, I've made my mind up, and I say, Amen! – a bit.

Well I sat back and thought a while,
    then tried a different ploy,
Now, Lord, I said, the Good Book says
    that Christians live in joy.
That's true, he said, you need the joy
    to bear the pain and sorrow,
So do you want to follow me, I said, Amen! – tomorrow.

Tomorrow, Lord, I'll say it then, that's when I'll say Amen,
I need to get it clear, can I just run through that again?
You say that I will need the joy to bear the pain and sorrow,
Well, yes, I think I've got it straight, I'll say, Amen – tomorrow.

He said, Look, I'm not asking you to spend an hour with me,
A quick salvation sandwich and a cup of sanctity,
The cost is you, not half of you, but every single bit,
Now tell me, will you follow me? I said, Amen! I quit.
I'm very sorry, Lord, I said, I'd like to follow you,
But I don't think religion is a manly thing to do.

He said, Forget religion then, and think about my Son,
And tell me if you're man enough to do what he has done.
Are you man enough to see the need, and man enough to go,
Man enough to care for those whom no one wants to know,
Man enough to say the thing that people hate to hear,
To battle through Gethsemane in loneliness and fear.
And listen! Are you man enough to stand it at the end,
The moment of betrayal by the kisses of a friend,
Are you man enough to hold your tongue,
    and man enough to cry,
When nails break your body – are you man enough to die?
Man enough to take the pain, and wear it like a crown,
Man enough to love the world and turn it upside down,
Are you man enough to follow me, I ask you once again?
I said, Oh, Lord, I'm frightened, but I also said Amen.
Amen, Amen, Amen, Amen; Amen, Amen, Amen,
I said, O Lord, I'm so frightened, but I also said, Amen.

HALLELUJAH IN THE BACK OF MY MIND

I take my problems to the altar, but my steps begin to falter,
And I feel as if I'm starting to fall,
For it's hard to recollect the proper way to genuflect
Upon arrival in a Pentecostal hall.
And I really want to share it, but I know they'll never wear it,
And the question in my head is underlined,
But just as I am saying, 'Who on earth invented praying?'
Hallelujah in the back of my mind.

There are some who have you kneeling,
    there are those who hit the ceiling,
There are others who insist on a smell,
There are some who keep their hats on,
    and a very few are bats on,
Having serpents in the service as well.
There are those who call you sinner
    if you dare enjoy your dinner,
And Gomorrah's in a half a glass of wine,
But just as I am sure I can't survive it any more,
Hallelujah in the back of my mind.

There are many, many people, who rely upon a steeple,
To remind them that they're aiming at God,
While some discover Zion under corrugated iron,
And they none of them believe they are odd,
So I take it and I shake it and I really try to break it,
And I think that I can leave it behind,

But just as I've dismissed it, there's a sound, I can't resist it,
Hallelujah in the back of my mind.

There's a man who when I'm sickly says,
    'You very, very quickly
Should be starting to get better, not worse,'
And he tells me that he sees
    I'm needing longer on my knees,
And there will always be a relevant verse.
But some say if you suffer, then your spirit will get tougher,
So you'd better find a will and get it signed,
But just as I'm refusing to go on, it's so confusing,
Hallelujah in the back of my mind.

Well, they say, 'Oh yes, you may do what you feel
    because it's real,
And everybody must be perfectly free,
And I'm happy to advise you, not a soul will criticise you,
Just as long as you are copying me.'
For they know the congregation in their own denomination
Is the nearest thing to heaven you could find,
But when I say, 'That's it! Oh, Lord, I know I'll never fit,'
Hallelujah in the back of my mind.

Hallelujah in the back of my mind
Hallelujah in the back of my mind
I've got to hand it to you, Lord,
You're really coming through,
With Hallelujah in the back of my mind.

THE REAL PROBLEM

Sunday is a funny day,
It starts with lots of noise.
Mummy rushes round with socks,
And Daddy shouts, 'You boys!'

Then Mummy says, 'Now don't blame them,
You know you're just as bad,
You've only just got out of bed,
It really makes me mad!'

My mummy is a Christian,
My daddy is as well,
My mummy says, 'Oh, heavens!'
My daddy says, 'Oh, hell!'

And when we get to church at last,
It's really very strange,
'Cos Mum and Dad stop arguing,
And suddenly they change.

At church my mum and dad are friends,
They get on very well,
But no one knows they've had a row,
And I'm not gonna tell.

People often come to them,
Because they seem so nice,
And Mum and Dad are very pleased
To give them some advice.

They tell them Christian freedom
Is worth an awful lot,
But I don't know what freedom means
If freedom's what they've got.

Daddy loves the meetings,
He's always at them all,
He's learning how to understand
The letters of St Paul.

But Mummy says, 'I'm stuck at home
To lead my Christian life,
It's just as well for blinkin' Paul
He didn't have a wife.'

I once heard my mummy say
She'd walk out of his life,
I once heard Daddy say to her
He'd picked a rotten wife.

They really love each other,
I really think they do.
I think the people in the church
Would help them – if they knew

WHY DID HE CHOOSE?

What a mountain climber this Jesus might have been,
Climbing through the shadows of the scariest ravine,
Coming through and resting where the air is cold and clean,
What a mountain climber this Jesus might have been.

So why did he choose
Death on a hillside,
Agony under a merciless sky,
When he could have stayed home,
Could have played with the thunder
Was I really the reason he decided to die?

What a stylish dancer this Jesus might have been,
Moving sweetly on the Galilean clubbing scene,
Dancing like a fire through the red and gold and green,
What a stylish dancer this Jesus might have been.

So why did he choose
Death on a hillside,
Agony under a merciless sky,
When he could have stayed home,
Could have played with the thunder
Was I really the reason he decided to die?

What a famous lover this Jesus might have been,
Up there with the others on the giant silver screen,
Showing all the ladies what a kiss could really mean,
What a famous lover this Jesus might have been.

So why did he choose
Death on a hillside,
Agony under a merciless sky,
When he could have stayed home,
Could have played with the thunder
Was I really the reason he decided to die?

What a leg-spin bowler this Jesus might have been,
A holy Rowley Jenkins on some Jewish village green,
Curling like a snake, and taking five for seventeen,
What a leg-spin bowler this Jesus might have been.

So why did he choose
Death on a hillside,
Agony under a merciless sky,
When he could have stayed home,
Could have played with the thunder
Was I really the reason he decided to die?

What a loving father this Jesus might have been,
Walking by his lady with the children in between,
Something in their faces that I have never seen,
What a loving father this Jesus might have been.

So why did he choose
Death on a hillside,
Agony under a merciless sky,
When he could have stayed home,
Could have played with the thunder
Was I really the reason he decided to die?

DAFFODILS

Daffodils are not flowers.
They are natural neon from the dark earth,
Precious metal grown impatient,
Beaten, shaped, and dipped in pools
Of ancient, sunken light.
Folded, packed, and parachuted through,
To stand and dumbly trumpet out
The twice triumphant sun.

NATHAN RAP

It was evening in the palace when the prophet came by,
There was trouble in his manner, there was thunder in his eye,
He was still for a moment, he was framed in the door,
And the king said, 'Nathan! . . . What are you here for?'
The prophet said, 'David, I've a tale to tell,'
So the king sat and listened as the darkness fell,
While the hard-eyed prophet took a seat and began,
The story of a merciless and evil man.

'This man,' said Nathan, 'had a mountain of gold,
Sheep by the thousand he bought and sold,
He never said,"Can I afford it or not?"'
What this man wanted, this man got!
And one thing he wanted, and he wanted real bad,
Was the only living thing that a poor man had,
And he knew that it was wrong, but he took it just the same.'
'I'll kill him!' said the king, 'Just tell me his name!'

'It was a lamb,' said the prophet, 'just a little baby lamb,
But he saw it and he took it and he didn't give a damn,
And he knew that it was special, and he knew it was a friend,
And he knew about the sadness that would never, never end,
And that same man began to plan a far more evil thing.'
Then David rose and cried aloud, 'He'll reckon with the king!'
'So do you think,' said Nathan,
    'we should stop his little game?'
'I'll smash him!' shouted David, 'tell me his name!'

44

'Be careful,' said the prophet, 'don't go overboard.'
For David's eyes were shining like the blade of a sword,
'Perhaps you should be merciful, perhaps you should try
To understand the man before you say he must die.'
But David said, 'I understand that wrong is always wrong,
I am the king, I must defend the weak against the strong.'
Then Nathan questioned softly,
    'So this man must take the blame?'
And the king was screaming,
    'Nathan! Will you tell me his name?'

Then a silence fell upon them like the silence of a tomb,
The prophet nodded slowly as he moved across the room,
And, strangely, as he came he seemed more awesome
    and more wise,
And when he looked at David there was sadness in his eyes.
But David's anger burned in him,
    he drew his sword and said,
'I swear, before the dawn has come, that sinner will be dead!
No more delay, no mercy talk, give me his name!' he cried,
Then Nathan said, 'It's you, it's you!' and the king just died.

I WANT TO BE WITH YOU

When the steamer has sailed
And my journey has failed
When the switches are on
But the power has gone
When I open my eyes
But the sun doesn't rise
When it's dark on the screen
Where the picture has been
When there's nobody there
To pretend that they care
When it comes to the end
And I long for a friend
When I wish that I knew
What is certain and true
I want to be with you

When I reach for the phone
But it's as dead as a stone
When the people I've known
Have gone and left me alone
When the things that I said
Are sounding empty and dead
When my talk about God
Is sounding foolish and odd
When the thoughts in my mind
Have left my feelings behind

When the skin on my hand
Is as dry as the sand
When the ache in my heart
Begins to tear me apart
Will I know what to do?
I want to be with you

When the silence has come
And the singers are dumb
When we stand in the light
And it's pointless to fight
When I see what they find
In the back of my mind
When there's no-one to blame
For the sin and the shame
As I wait for the word
To let me fly like a bird
But I fear in my heart
I wouldn't know how to start
When the tears in my eyes
Are blurring over the skies
When I suddenly claim
To remember your name
When I see that it's you
Coming out of the blue
Jesus, I want to be with you

Silences and Nonsenses

1990-1995

AM I THE ONLY ONE?

When I wrote *The Sacred Diary of Adrian Plass – aged 37¾* (originally a column in Family Magazine) I honestly did believe that I was the only Christian in the world who did such silly things and experienced such wild inconsistencies in his life and belief. Surely I must be the only one who had ever tried to make a paperclip move by faith? Could there be anyone else in the world who took far too many tablets to combat toothache and claimed that he was avoiding the dentist as a matter of faith rather than fear?

Responses to that book showed to my great relief that I was far from being the only one, and much of the poetry and verse in this section reflects my amazed discovery that the truth (in any area of life) really can set people free. The Christian church is particularly bedeviled by an insistence on corporate truth that excludes honest debate about what actually happens to ordinary, flawed people like myself in the course of day-to-day living. God must tear his hair out – never mind, he's got plenty if the old masters got it right.

What a mixture I find in this list. *Graces* is made up of three very slight verses, originating in a request from our local publicans for a rhyming grace to be said at their annual dinner. I got a bit carried away after that, I'm afraid. By contrast, *Dear Family* is an agonised message to my children, apologising for demons and devils of my past that might have affected them as they grew up.

Heaven and *I Mothered She* are two of my own favourites, perhaps because the subjects are so important to me, and *Cricket* – well, it's just an impassioned cry from the heart. Come on, Lord, get the rollers out, mark the pitch, put a couple of angels on to making cucumber sandwiches. You can bat first.

1990–1995

MINISTRY

I want to have a ministry,
I want to be profound,
I want to see the folks I touch,
Go spinning to the ground.
I want to use a funny voice,
Mysterious and low,
I want to spot uneven legs,
I want to watch them grow.
I want to have a little team,
No more than two or three,
A totally devoted group,
Whose ministry is *me*.
They'd keep an eye upon my soul,
And tell me how it looks,
And even more importantly,
They'd sell my tapes and books.

I want to send my prayer list out,
Full colour ones look flash,
The ones that say,
'I'm greatly blessed,
And could you send some cash?'
I'd send them out by first-class post,
And please the folk who got 'em,
By putting little written bits,
In biro, at the bottom.

I want to be a humble star,
At major church events,
And lead obscure seminars,
In great big leaky tents.
I want to say how I deplore,
The famous Christian hunters,
I want to sign their Bibles,
And refer to them as 'punters'.

I really want a ministry,
I want to alter lives,
I want to pray for something dead,
And see if it revives.
I do, I want a ministry,
I'm sure it's all been planned,
I'll make a start as soon as God,
Removes the job in hand.

CRICKET

I'm dying to live after living has ended,
I'm living for life after death,
Alive to the fact that I'm dead apprehensive,
I'll live to the end of my breath.
But what would life be were I no longer living,
And death was no longer alive,
How would I stick it without any cricket,
How would I ever survive?
Would I cross swords on some heavenly Lords,
With the angels of Holding and Hall,
Would I face up to Lillee without feeling silly,
And even catch sight of the ball?
Would a man with a beard whom the bowlers all feared,
Redeem us from losing – a sin?
Yes, by Grace we'd be saved as his century paved,
The way to a glorious win.
I promise you, Lord, I'll never get bored,
I'll practice the harp, there, I've sworn,
If cricket's allowed, I'll be back on my cloud,
The moment that stumps have been drawn

CREED

I cannot say my creed in words,
How should I spell despair, excitement, joy and grief,
Amazement, anger, certainty and unbelief?
What was the grammar of those sleepless nights?
Who the subject, what the object
Of a friend who will not come, or does not come
And then creates his own eccentric special dawn,
A blinding light that does not blind?
Why do I find you in the secret wordless places
Where I hide from your eternal light?
I hate you, love you, miss you, wish that you would go,
And yet I know that long ago you made a fairy tale for me,
About the day when you would take your sword
And battle through the thicket of the things I have become.
You'll kiss to life my sleeping beauty
    waiting for her prince to come.
Then I will wake and look into your eyes and understand
And for the first time I will not be dumb
And I shall say my creed in words.

DIET

expansion was not good business for my body
then I replaced the four sugars in my tea
with sweeteners no after taste eh funny
fat out fibre shovelled in or through
got a shade depressed a little blue
a friend told me alcohol inflates
gave up claret very nearly died
no more booze nothing fried
full of tuna fish and dates
planned to cheat but then
a miracle I saw my feet
like other better men
fresh air was sweet
and nature smiled
I ran and leapt
soundly slept
happy child
so serene
so lean
a bit
fit

I
ate
a bit
a treat
or trophy
had a steak
a titchy cake
a glass of port
a prize I thought
for dieting so well
oh I smiled as I fell
suddenly I wanted chop
crazy eyed I hit the shops
syrup jam and lemon cheese
do spring into my trolley please
doughnuts plumply filled with jam
cover me with sticky sugar here I am
chocolate fancy chocolate milk or plain
trace the orbit of my lusting mouth again
crinkly scrummy scrunchy deep fried chips
how I yearn to squeeze you firmly in my lips
expansion was not good business for my body

POOR SAD CHILD (for two voices)

Poor sad child
        poor child
poor boy
        poor girl
don't run, don't run away
                        don't hide
we love you
        we're sorry
we let you down
            we left you
we settled for too little
                    we were frightened
of your pain
        pain is better buried, we thought
but we were wrong
        so wrong
to leave you there
        leave you wondering if tears can ever really dry
we threw our lot in with the half alive
                            half alive
but now
        now we've come to find you
we can face you now
            we so longed to see your face
we want to see you smile
            see you smile

dear child
dear child
be our child
   our child again
we've brought a friend
            a friend who changes things
he's with us now, his name
            his name is Jesus
Jesus – he can heal you
            he can make you smile again
You'll love him
      we love him
            he loves you
so much
   so much
      so much
poor sad child.

NEW TO ME

New to me
But old in years
When he came
Examined tears.
Antique love
Regard me now
Love so good
Kiss my brow.
Complete release
Chance to start
Eventually
Forgive my heart.
Now the peace
Waits for me
Rest in hope
Maybe free

ARTS GROUP

Our local Christian Arts group meets at St Virginia's Hall,
The cost is not prohibitive, you pay a pound, that's all.
It started last September and it's been tremendous fun,
We meet alternate Fridays
    and we share what we have done.
Comments must be true or kind for nobody is barred,
They range from, 'Oh, that's really good,'
    to 'Gosh, you have worked hard!'

There's Mrs Leith from Brassey Heath,
    divorced, but never low,
Whose bosom mountainously shrouds
    the fires down below.
Her many giant canvases are mostly purple sky,
She paints in tinted marmite – no,
    we've never asked her why.
At home her neon works of art are hanging high and low,
We've often wondered why her husband took so long to go.

Miss Duncalk from Cheyney Walk is very thin and tense,
She was a Carl Andre fan,
    she thought his bricks made sense.
She educates our appetites with extracts from Camus,
She says we get a lot from it, we all pretend we do.
In matters of philosophy she briskly puts us right,
We hope her inner comprehension
    keeps her warm at night.

Mr Grange is slightly strange, he's something small in eggs,
He always says 'the yolk's on me,' and looks at ladies' legs.
He brings along his only sketch, it's called *Reclining Nude*,
He says it is aesthetic, but it's not, it's very rude.
Mrs Blair, our acting chair, says, 'Yes, he's less than sound,
But unlike some more pure in heart,
   he always pays his pound.'

Mr Smee is ninety-three, but vibrant and alive,
He's never late, unlike his mate, who died in sixty-five.
He plays the bongos badly, at a quite frenetic rate,
It lasts for several minutes, you just have to sit and wait.
Mrs Leith says, through her teeth, 'I cannot take much more,
If left to me, then Mr Smee would not reach ninety-four.'

The sisters Verne are very stern, they always think the same,
They tell us Joyce is vulgar, and Picasso is a shame.
Wordsworth was a pantheist, Lawrence was depraved,
Muggeridge was not too bad, but was he *really* saved?
C.S Lewis wasn't quite a fundamentalist,
And Dylan Thomas? Hopeless,
   he was permanently intoxicated.

Last week our members all agreed
    that we should make a start,
On planning some more public way to share abroad our art.
And so the works of Leith and Blair,
    and Grange and Voke and me,
Will grace the public library for all the world to see.
What greater satisfaction than to help the unsaved find,
A glimpse through our creations
    of the great creator's mind?

WHEN I WAS SMALL

When I was small
I didn't know the world had fallen long ago
I stumbled often, fell from trees
Enjoyed the pride of bloodied knees
And banks were made for rolling down
Or sliding when the snow had come
My bones would bend more easily
Even when they broke they mended soon
And people gave me things to cheer me up.
I once went sledging with a friend at night
He didn't trust the moon and he was right
It slipped away as we began our ride
But I was glad, I loved the dark
For all I cared we could have sledged into eternity
I wished that pale hissing dream would never end
It did – I have the scars
I still have all the scars from all the falls
And mainly on my knees
But somewhere deep inside, where no-one ever sees
I have some other scars that never do completely
    seem to heal
The cause of them I cannot now recall, but then,
I didn't know the world had fallen long ago
When I was small.

JENNY

Our Father who art in heaven
Jenny walked in front of a train last night
Hallowed be thy name, thy Kingdom come
She was only thirty-seven
Thy will be done on earth, as it is in heaven
You knew what she was going to do, didn't you, Lord?
Give us this day our daily bread
She had no hope left
And forgive us our trespasses as we forgive those who
trespass against us
Jenny is forgiven, isn't she?
Lead us not into temptation
Lots of us are on the edge of darkness
And deliver us from evil
The only strength we have is yours
For thine is the Kingdom
And she's living there now
The power and the glory
She's yours, Lord
For ever and ever
Jenny
Amen

ANGEL

Six o'clock, the sky that evening
Autumn grey, a shining dome
The sun a glowing tangerine
That rolled along the far horizon
Don't remember where I'd been
He was just a shabby figure standing by the roadside
   near my home.
I parked the car and stood awhile,
   enjoyed the way October daylight sweetly, sadly dies
Then turned and walked towards the stranger
Don't know why
Except that when I passed I'd seen a warm
   and strange expression in his eyes
When I asked where he was going he just smiled and said,
   'Well now my friend,
I don't believe I know,
But that's no reason not to go unless you need me.'
'Come eat with me and stay awhile,
There's food for two, the sofa makes a fair to average bed.'
He said, 'Okay,' we went inside,
   I lit the lamps and poured some wine
We talked, and soon some orphan hope
   broke down the wall
And wept through every stumbling word of mine.

How the darkness circled round us
Like a disappointed foe.
It crouched and waited hungrily,
It filled the space behind the lamplight,
We were safe inside the glow.
And the wine was more than nectar,
    blood red in the gleaming of the fire
His touch upon the bread disturbed me,
    something far beyond recall, or underground,
Then a smiling benediction seemed to fall
And work a little miracle,
    a relaxation in my heart. I heard a sound
My own voice, live with wakened passion,
    breaking with a nameless yearning
Like a long-forsaken child
    who is sick of running wild in desert places.
'Where's your home?' I asked, 'perhaps one day
I'll visit you.' His eyes were burning coals,
    he whispered, 'Yes, I hope you will.'
We said goodnight, he slept, I wandered out,
    the air was cold and clean
And looking up for one eternal moment
I felt homesick for a place I'd never seen.

Later, when the dawn was breaking
Later, when the day was there
When I awoke in sore distress
To find the morning grey and silver
I was quick to rise and dress
Almost ran towards the stairway,
  hoping that my friend would still be there.
But far away, and in my mind, I seemed to hear
  a distant ocean sighing to the shore
A sound like giant wings in motion.
Down below
The sheets and rugs were piled neatly,
  too much money lay beside the door.
Though I called out through the doorway
  in my heart I knew he must be gone
The silence was profound
And the countryside around was cold and empty.
'Just one more day,' I said, 'he could have stayed.
To leave so soon with countless questions
  waiting to be asked.'
I closed the door, inside the fire was dead,
  but in the silent air
A gentle warmth caressed the autumn morning
As it glowed and loved and softly lingered there.

And the words he spoke that evening
Were so full of love and light
That the agony inside me
Was attacked and put to flight.
And you may believe I'm crazy
And I may believe you're right,
But I think it was an angel
That I entertained that night.

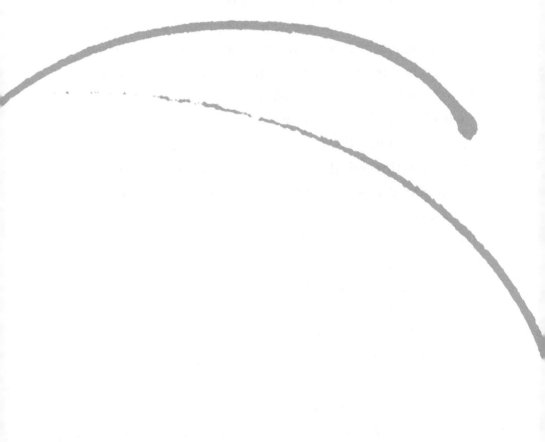

ANGLICAN RAP

Let's kneel, let's stand,
Let's be terribly bland,
Let's sing quite loud with a dignified clap,
Let's process around the church in a victory lap.
Check us on the old denominational map,
From the Isle of Wight to the Watford Gap,
Everybody's doing it – the Anglican rap.
Come along and boogie to the Anglican beat,
Just grab your hermeneutics and exegete!

Take a cruise to the pews, have a snooze, read the news,
Don't go looking for disaster with a Pentecostal pastor,
There'll be tongues and revelations
   with bizarre interpretations.
Don't smile when life's vile in the house church style,
Or muddle through the mist with a modern Methodist
Do you fancy looking barmy with the silly Sally Army?
Don't meet above the bakers
   with the Shakers and the Quakers,
Or shiver in the water like the Baptists say you oughter,
We don't baptise in the bottom of a tank,
Our font is Norman and our vicar is Frank.
We're well aware of current theological trends,
But Frank and Norman are still good friends.
We're trendy and we're modish,
   have you seen our groovy cassocks?
And we're open to the option of inflated rubber hassocks.

Be a real cool cat, be an Anglican dude,
Every now and then we're *almost* rude.

Let's kneel, let's stand,
Let's be terribly bland,
Let's sing quite loud with a dignified clap,
Let's process around the church in a victory lap.
Check us on the old denominational map,
From the Isle of Wight to the Watford Gap,
Everybody's doing it – the Anglican rap.
Come along and boogie to the Anglican beat,
Just grab your hermeneutics and exegete!

Don't falter at the altar, have a rave in the nave,
Have a smile in the aisle, have a lapse in the apse,
Have a thriller by the pillar, eat an apple in the chapel,
Have some oysters in the cloisters,
    read some Auden to the warden,
Climb the font if you want, feel the power up the tower,
Light a torch in the porch, start a fire in the choir,
Raise your arms in the psalms,
    mind the gorgon at the organ,
Swap your knickers for the vicar's,
    check you're zipped in the crypt.
Some of us speak through tightly clenched teeth,
And lots of us look like Edward Heath
    (and that's just the ladies)
Anglicans hurry to the old God shack,
To be first in the queue for the seats at the back.

We're a very broad church, we're home from home,
You can chat up the vicar, or flirt with Rome.
Our leader isn't certain if he's comin' or he's goin'
He's a great big hairy fellow and his name is Rowan

Let's kneel, let's stand,
Let's be terribly bland,
Let's sing quite loud with a dignified clap,
Let's process around the church in a victory lap.
Check us on the old denominational map,
From the Isle of Wight to the Watford Gap,
Everybody's doing it – the Anglican rap.
Come along and boogie to the Anglican beat,
Just grab your hermeneutics and exegete!

SACRED HEART

On that day his father turned from him
For in his sacred heart
He headed up the holocaust
Perpetrated endless petty meannesses
On Sunday afternoons in Peckham Rye
Murdered frightened children on the moors
Didn't give the mower back
Calmly supervised the killing fields
Cheated British Rail
He watched the blank-eyed starving babies die
And sulked because there was no ginger ale
Perfect circles
Do not think they end
Do not think they start
Think only that he holds us all
Within his sacred heart

I MOTHERED SHE

I mothered she who mothered me,
The body that I never knew,
(Though she knew mine so well when I was small
   and she was all my need)
So plaintive now,
Her arms surrendered high to be undressed or dressed,
Like some poor sickly child,
Who sees no shame in helplessness.
And yet, when I collapsed and cried beside her on the bed,
She was my mother once again,
She reached her hand out to the child in me,
She dried my tears
And held me there till I was still.
So ill, so long
Until, at last,
   when endless days of hopefulness had faded finally
There came a night of harmony, a night of many psalms,
I mothered she who mothered me
And laid my sister gently
In our Father's arms.

AM I THE ONLY ONE?

Am I the only one
Who follows God
Nottingham Forest
Neighbours
And his own inclinations – usually in reverse order?
I do hope not.

Am I the only one
Who likes Norman Wisdom films
Bat out of Hell
Little House on the Prairie
And *Silence of the Lambs*?
Probably.

Am I the only one
Who hasn't learnt to drive
Probably never will
Doesn't want to
And might well murder the next person who asks why not?
Maybe.

Am I the only one
Who checks his carpet for big bits before hoovering it
Then afterwards finds the suction pipe blocked with dead dogs
Half bricks, rolls of prairie wire, nests of tiddly winks
Most of the *Sunday Times* and six pounds fifty in small change
I doubt it.

Am I the only one
Who talks loudly to himself when he's alone
Then suddenly realises he isn't
Feels like a loony
And tries to make it sound like a song?
Surely not.

Am I the only one
Who hates all criticism
Especially the constructive sort
Because that usually means
I have to do something about it?
I don't think so.

Am I the only one
Who likes to have his cake
Eat it
Sick it up
Then feel sorry for himself?
Possibly.

Am I the only one
Who loves and needs love
And fails and falls and cries
And takes the hand of anyone whose turn it is to be strong
Whose turn it is to be Jesus for me?
Am I the only one?

BIBLES AND RIFLES

Bibles and rifles
Handled by amateurs
Paper and metal
Tear us apart.
Fixing their sights
On the heart of reality
Bibles and rifles
There from the start.
Rifles and Bibles
Crashing through history
Leather and wood
Wounding and tears
Aiming and blaming
Shattering mystery
Rifles and Bibles
Ring in our ears
Bibles and trifles
Foibles and rifles
Rifles and Bibles
Bibles and rifles
Handled by amateurs
Ring in our ears.

DEAR FAMILY

Dear family, I write to you in this campfire place
Where temporary flames repel the savage things
Whose glowing hungry eyes appear from time to time.
They know, as I do, that a campfire only burns
as long as fuel lasts.
My stocks are low as ever, and these devils never rest.
But I have light and time enough to write to you
Dear family, asleep, for once, beside me here in peace,
To say how I regret the need to share
such fearful travelling with you.
I know that monster-ridden darkness is my own affair
I have no right to take you there.
The battle I shall face tonight will threaten you
But certainly it never was your fight.
God knows I wish that it was otherwise
That we could strike our camp and head for home.
I have some choice
But when those creatures leap I find I am clean out of choice
And they draw blood so easily.
Dear family, as you awake,
And eye my camp-fire ashes nervously
I want to say how I am wretchedly aware
That others would protect and lead you properly.
They would be strong and confident and sure
They would be many things that I will never be
I only know they could not love you more

GRACES

i) FOR PUBLICANS

Lord, we meet together here,
Mild and bitter, stout and pale.
Grant, from now till final orders
That our spirits never ail.
With specific gravity
We shall hock depravity,
Please fill each hungry cavity
Let gratitude prevail.

ii) FOR TAXI DRIVERS

Simple thanks we offer now,
No trace of ambiguity,
For once we'll take this humble fare
Expecting no gratuity

iii) FOR RAIL EMPLOYEES

Speed this food, Lord, as it comes
On its journey to our tums.
Let there be no long diversion
Of this edible excursion,
Unavoidably delayed
Just behind the shoulder-blade,
Or stranded in the lower back
By lettuce leaves upon the track.
May all traffic safely pass
And our digestions be first-class.

GETTING THERE

Once I've cleaned this house up properly,
I honestly think I'll get somewhere.
Once I've pulled out every single piece of furniture
And used an abrasive cloth with strong stuff on it,
I think I shall come to grips with the rest of my life.
Once I've put everything into separate piles,
Each containing the same sort of thing
   (if you know what I mean)
I think I'll manage.
Once I've written a list that includes absolutely everything,
I think the whole business will seem very much clearer.
Once I've had time to work slowly from one item to another,
I'm sure things will change
Once I've eaten sensibly for more than a week and a half
Once I've sorted out the things that are my fault,
Once I've sorted out the things that are not my fault,
Once I've spent a little more time reading useful books,

Being with people I like,
Getting out into the air,
Making bread,
Drinking less,
Drinking more,
Going to the theatre,
Adopting a third-world child,
Eating free-range eggs,
And writing long letters,
Once I've pulled every single piece of furniture right out,
And cleaned this house up properly,
Once I've become somebody else,
I honestly think I'll get somewhere.

HILLS OF HOME

Some other country
Claims me now
But I will stay
Because we love this place,
And I can always see the hills of home
From top-floor windows
But only if I climb the stairs.
I'd rather see the hills
Than say my prayers
At the bottom of the stairs.
Some other country
Lacking this beloved citizen
Whose straining eyes
Have never even seen the land where he belongs,
Except for distant hills
From top floor windows,

When he climbs the stairs
With others who might share
Unwillingness to mumble prayers
At the bottom of the stairs.
Some other country
Where the builder waits
And faithfully prepares
The mansions we shall need,
All set among the hills
And all of them are made by hand
And all of them are home
And all of them are visited
And none of them need stairs

LANDING

I understand a fear of flying,
Not much fun if things go wrong up there,
Options narrow down to less than two,
But I enjoy the peace of being nowhere,
Fending off the food, sleeping through the film,
Hating first-class passengers,
Solving, yet again, the puzzle of the toilet doors.
Best of all is being sure that those I left behind,
Are left behind, and not about to suddenly appear,
While those who wait will have to wait a while,
For words and nods and smiles of understanding,
They are there and I am here,
Suspended, dreaming, guiltless in the air.
My fear is not of flying but of landing.

WORRY

No burglars came again last night
Just as they failed to come the night before,
    and for all the nights I can remember
No burglars yet again although I listened, as I always do, for them
Once more they did not oil and ease the rusty bolt that
    holds the garden gate
Behind the shed beside the house
Nor did I hear them moving in the yard
    at some heart-sobbing wretched hour
It was the ticking of a clock upon my wall
That sounded like the pad of evil steps a hundred feet away
They did not creep inside, their blind-from-birth brutality
    reduced to stealth and whispers
They did not stand above me.
Were not there with threats and ugly promises, intoxicated
    by the scent of fear incontinent
Nor did they then, with weapons that I meekly placed into
    their hands, proceed to sever from my chilled insides the
    screaming child who has evaded birth for so long now
They did not come

They were not there again last night.
And what if they should never come?
Such a waste of nights
I might have slept
But if I had, I feel quite sure
They would have come
Those burglars – oh, yes, they would have come

GENERATIONS

I took my daughter to the park last night
She ran with a shout to the roundabout
The roundabout went round and round
But it never stopped anywhere very profound
It just went round and round and round
It just went round and round

I took my daughter to the park last night
She bounced like a spring to the grown-up swing
It swung quite high and it swung quite low
But there wasn't any doubt where the swing would go
It just swung high and it just swung low,
It just swung high and low.

I took my daughter to the park last night
Her eyes grew wide when she saw the slide
She climbed the steps and she slid back down
But the same sun set on the same old town
She just climbed up and she just slid down
Just climbed and slid back down.

We're all going down to the park tonight
Where the swings go high and the swings go low
But there isn't any doubt where the swings will go
And you climb the steps and you sit back down
While the same sun sets on the same old town
Where the roundabout just goes round and round.
And never stops anywhere very profound
It just goes round and round and round,
It just goes round and round

CHRISTMAS

Christmas happens anyway
    – it happened in our house today,
It's good! And yet,
    I have to say, for me there's something missing.
It's not that Santa didn't come;
    he floated past our worldly locks,
He drank his sherry,
    ate his pie, left me a pair of purple socks,
And lots of other things.
My daughter gave me half a beetle in a box,
    a touching sacrifice.
There's no significance, I hope,
    in all the gifts of scent and soap,
In Dumbledore and Hagrid Shapes!
And who sent exercising tapes?
That isn't very nice.
My son said, 'Dad, I've spent a lot,
A portable word processor.'
I really was excited till I got,
My pencil in a plastic pot.
But there were toys and Garfield mugs
And boxer-shorts and laughs and hugs,
And anyway, they always say,
    the thought's the thing that really counts.
There's something missing, and it isn't here.
    I'm not sure what it is.

The crib confuses me because – I see it as it surely was,
Divine confusion,
    shepherds visiting the new-born shepherd,
Mary proud but puzzled, Joseph close, concerned for her,
And what would tiny babies want with gold and
    frankincense and myrrh?
Why did a million angels fill the sky,
    like snowflakes on a starry night?
I guess that no-one quite knew what was going on,
Except that something right was happening,
And God was saying, and is saying still,
'Here is my son, do with him as you will.
Though you may kill him he will live for you forever now,
Not lost in rhymes or mimes or special times,
But in the human heart, where revolutions really start,
And struggles in the darkness never seem to cease.
He offered then, he offers now,
    the only gift you'll ever want or need,
The possibility of peace.'

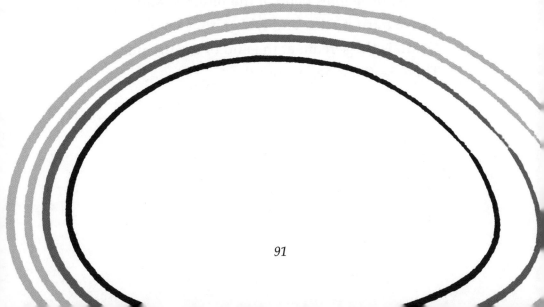

DEATH

What do we do about death?
We don't
The monster is hidden away
It's not in the zoo for the public to view
The look on its face would empty the place
We don't want to die! the people would cry
Death is the curse in the back of the hearse
We don't need to see it today.

What do we do about death?
We don't
We shovel it under the ground
Under the sod, and hope there's a God
Whose principles bend at the bitterest end
Or we burn it away and whispering say
Death is the scream at the end of the dream
There isn't a lonelier sound.

What do we do about death?
We don't
We don't even give it a name
He's gone before to a distant shore
She's passed away, we gloomily say
He's fallen asleep in a terminal heap
Death is the spear that is poisoned with fear
It pierces the heart of the game.

What do we do about death?
We don't
But once in the angry sun
A winner was slain at the centre of pain
When a battle was fought at the final resort
But because of the cross it was fought without loss
And death is the knife that will free us for life
Because of what Jesus has done.

HEAVEN

When I'm in heaven
Tell me there'll be kites to fly
The kind they say you can control
Although I never did for long
The kind that spin and spin and spin and spin
Then sulk and dive and die
And rise again and spin again
And dive and die and rise up yet again
I love those kites

When I'm in heaven
Tell me there'll be friends to meet
In ancient oak-beamed Sussex pubs
Enfolded by the wanton Downs
And summer evenings lapping lazily against the shore
Of sweet familiar little lands
Inhabited by silence or by nonsenses
The things you cannot safely say in any other place
I love those times

When I'm in heaven
Tell me there'll be seasons when the colours fly
Poppies splashing flame
Through dying yellow, living green
And autumn's burning sadness
   that has always made me cry
For things that have to end

For winter fires that blaze like captive suns
But look so cold when morning comes
I love the way the seasons change

When I'm in heaven
Tell me there'll be peace at last
That in some meadow filled with sunshine
Filled with buttercups and filled with friends
You'll chew a straw and fill us in on how things really are
And if there is some harm in laying earthly hope
    at heaven's door
Or in this saying so
Have mercy on my foolishness, dear Lord
I love this world you made – it's all I know

HEAVEN: EXTRA CHRISTMAS VERSE

When I'm in heaven
Tell me there'll be Christmases without the pain
No memories that will not fade
No chilled and sullen sense of loss
That cannot face the festive flame
Nor breathe excitement from the ice-cream air
Tell me how the things that Christmas should have been
Will be there for eternity in one long peaceful dawn
For all of us to share
I always loved the promises of Christmas

Silences and Nonsenses

1995-2000

LEARNING TO FLY

I enjoyed writing most of these poems. A little imp used to sit on my shoulder muttering into my ear that I wasn't really a writer, and that I was bound to be sussed eventually by the grown-ups. During this period he seemed to have abandoned his miserable mission, temporarily at any rate. *Learning to Fly* appeared in a book of the same name, a combination of pictures and poems produced in collaboration with my friend Ben Ecclestone, who has also illustrated several of my books over the years. We had great fun with this project. Some of the poems from the book, *Wild Affairs, Winchester Cathedral, Mother, Playground* and *I Cannot Make You Love me*, were a real joy to write, and it was genuinely exciting to see the brilliant paintings with which Ben made the book such a visual feast. Our second collection, *Words From The Cross*, moves in illustration and poetry through the words spoken by Jesus from the cross, as recorded in the Gospels, and are included here in their original order.

Some of the other poems in this list are singular, if not odd. *The Agony of Painlessness* is an evocation of the kind of rubbishy verse we turned out by the bucketload in the sixties, the dominant feature being a determination to be in diametric opposition to the status quo, even if it changed. You just moved round a bit. *United in Glory* is one of my favourite poems to read out loud, not least because the final line ensures a laugh in just about every setting I can think of. I freely concede that *Andromeda Veal to the Pope* looks a little strange out of context. This little girl, the main character in a book entitled *The Horizontal Epistles of Andromeda Veal* is stranded in hospital as her broken leg heals. She fills in her time by writing to a selection of famous people, including Margaret Thatcher, God, Cliff Richard and, in these lines of doggerel, the Pope. It may not be literature, but I just love Andromeda. For Bridget and I *Playground* has become a favourite for finishing off live evenings. Reading it makes us happy.

I hope you get as much pleasure from reading this mixed bunch as I did from writing them.

LEARNING TO FLY

We have stretched our arms towards him
We have longed to draw him down
Sought to raise him from the frozen heart of stone,
We have searched the rocky passes
   with our sisters and our brothers,
We have raced through shadowed valleys of our own
And our fingertips have touched him,
Yes, our fingertips have touched him,
Though we move before his touch can slow us down,
How we grieve that in our turning,
The eternal moment passes,
As our newly floating hopes begin to drown.
And we long for when we rise with him,
Beyond this place of searching,
Moving effortlessly through the new-made sky,
Where the blue could not be deeper,
And a child's sun is smiling,
On the citizens of heaven as they fly.
Then the rising will not lift us,
   nor the falling bring us down,
And the springs will ring with echoing delight,
But until we spread our wings in the company of angels,
Dancing is the nearest thing to flight.

WILD AFFAIRS

Should I have had more wild affairs
In old Cathedral towns
Before I got redeemed by God
And had to settle down?

Should I have touched more shining hair
And kissed more pretty eyes
Told through the soft and silky nights
More soft and silky lies?

Should I have crossed the muffled close
And known as evening fell
Through orange light on virgin snow
That all things could be well?

Should I have spent more glowing hours
Behind the leaded panes
Among the overcoats and scarves
The innocent refrains?

Should I have seen with calmer eyes
How tragedies begin
The darkness wrapped in cellophane
The warmth of joy and sin?

Should I have lingered in the streets
To say more morning prayers
As all the world went greyly past
Should I have echoed theirs?

Should I have learned to love the world
Before I let it go
The shadowed marks of many feet
Criss-crossing in the snow?

Should I have taken time to hear
More distant church bells ring
And marvelled at the kingdom
Long before I met the king?

JACQUELINE

For Jacqueline du Pré

Jacqueline, you learned to fly so young,
Flew so high, so far, so fast, so well,
I deal in words,
   but none of them could track your wild flight,
Nor formulate my sadness when you fell.

Jacqueline, I always watched your eyes,
You reached a world, I cannot fathom how,
Where earth and heaven joined
   in chords of surging harmony,
God grant you peace to fly there safely now.

ANGLICAN ALPHABET

A is for Anglican ladies in hats,
B is for Belfries where Bishops Breed Bats,
C is for Candles and Chapels and Choirs,
   Curates, Commissioners,
   Crooked Church spires,
   Crosses, Collections, and Change for the
   better,
D is for Dunking, though Baptists get wetter,
E is for Everyone does what he wants,
F is for Funerals, Follies, and Fonts,
G is for God and for Graveyard as well,
H is for Heaven and Heating and Hell,
I is for Icons and Inter-church whist,
J is for Jenkins, who may not exist,
K is for Kingdom, the King and his search,
L is for Leaving his Lambs in the Lurch,
M is for Matins and Mass and Modernity,
N is for Notices reaching eternity,
O is for Outreach and sowing the seed,
P is for Praise, which we don't seem to need,
Q is for Quiet-time (see the above),
R is for Raising the Roof with our love,
S is for Sin and Surprise and Salvation,
Synods and Sexual Orientation,
Suffering, Sadness, Sermons and Smells,
T is for Time and the Tolling of bells,
U is for Unity, one with another,

V is for Vicars who'd rather not bother,
W stands for a World in decline,
X is for Xmas, a promising sign,
Y is for Yobs
And Youth fellowships too,
Z is for all of us
Z is for Zoo.

FORGIVE US IF WE SAY

Forgive us if we say
We want to take you in our arms
Sad Father, weeping God
Breathless with the storms
Of anger, of compassion
Fists clenched hard around your grief
Around the marks
The cost
The proof
How can you give us up?
How can you hand us over?
Of course you never can
Never could
Never will
Burdened with perfection and with passion
Lay your head down
Let us hold you for a while
We will try to be to you
What you have been to us so many times
Peace, Lord, be a child once again
Do you remember Mary's arms?
So warm
So different

Rest quietly and soon you will be strong enough
To be a lion thundering from way beyond the east
We will come trembling from the west
We promise you
Like birds
Like doves
Like children who have suddenly remembered
Who taught them how to laugh
But just for now
Forgive us if we say
We want to take you in our arms
Sad Father, weeping God

GROWN-UPS

We search in vain for grown-ups
On mislaying childhood's gem
And tremble for our children,
When we find that we are them.

UNITED IN GLORY

Duncan Edwards, once the best,
Went early to his well-earned rest,
To find God nursed a secret dream,
Of managing a football team,
Seeing Munich made God sad,
But keen to rescue good from bad,
Couldn't help but be delighted,
Most of Manchester United,
Turned up at the Pearly Gates,
Good old Duncan with his mates,

They were offered free salvation,
Pending full negotiation,
Contracts stating that the fee,
Would bind them for eternity,
(Transfer bans were just as well,
The only place to go was hell)
Wages well worth playing for,
The love of God for ever more,

They practised kicks and moves and passes,
Over heaven's shining grasses,
God laid on boots and kit and towels,
But vetoed all professional fouls,
Aware the team was not complete,
He said he'd need to slightly cheat,
So, doing the pragmatic thing,
He put an angel on the wing.

At last, God's team lined up with pride,
To play Old Nick's infernal side,
And watched by several billion souls,
Heaven won by thirteen goals,
Duncan, who'd put seven in,
Asked God what made him sure they'd win,
Said God, 'No miracles required,
You did it all, a team inspired,
Besides, I knew that, as a rule,
Hell recruits from Liverpool.'

AUTUMN

Autumn is a fierce reply
To those who still deny your brooding heart
Flaming death in fading sun
The yearly mulching of elation, sadness, pain
A branch unclothed, the tatters flying
Rainbowed floating rain, tentatively lying
Far more beautiful for dying
The final breath, softly whispering 'enough'
But memories come down like leaves
On old uneven pathways
Such a sweetness
See, my breathing stands upon the air
And you, my oldest friend, are there
As evening falls we pass between the tall park gates
A shortcut to the town
A shiver moves the children's swings
The earth is soft and dark and rich
An early Christmas cake
We know the grass will not be cut again –
Not this year
So, down the tiled streets
The peopled rivulets
Perhaps towards some tea
In places that were ours but now have changed
Though early autumn darkness

Stares as hungrily through plate-glass windows
Velveted by bright electric embers
We are so glad to be there pouring tea
Pleased that we are laughing once again
Relieved that we are us once more
I have been troubled by a fear that everything is gone
The fingertips of friendship cold and numb
But autumn is a season that returns
With intimations of the death of pain
And so my friend shall we
Spirit, you have brooded well
Melancholy autumn beauty
And the spring to come

DEATH OF A TRAFFIC WARDEN

He stood at the crossroads of his own life
Directing the traffic of emotions, thoughts, events
Too watchful once, perhaps
For woe betide some maverick urge
    that tried to jump the queue
And overtake good common sense that ought to set the pace
He tried, he really tried to set his face against irregularity
Longed to see the day when all of life's unruly streams
Would be reorganised into an earthly paradise
    of dead straight lines
With no untidy tailbacks to upset him
Alas for all his dreams, his bosses wouldn't let him
He had three bosses
One in Heaven,
One in Hastings, one at home
The first and last of these instructed him in many things
They taught him that the waving through of tender thoughts
A blind eye turned when unashamed compassion
Does a sudden U-turn in the outside lane
Need not be crimes
That facts and feelings have to double-park sometimes
And in the end, in the main, love was flowing freely
Far too soon, far too soon for us, the traffic noises died
And on that soundless day
A chauffeur-driven certainty came softly in the morning
And carried him away.

SOWETO 1993

South Africa was lovely from the air
But as we spiralled to Johannesburg
We wondered why they'd let those fields of litter
Desecrate the landscape for so many miles
    around the city edge.
Perhaps they didn't care
Perhaps they found it easier to blank it out
Than bother to recycle it or bury it beneath the ground
But is there not a likelihood, we thought
That in the end the problem will grow mountainous
The stench of foul neglect become obscene
Until that mountain falls towards the city
Toppling irreversibly
And covering the part of town that prides itself
    on staying clean?

ANDROMEDA VEAL TO THE POPE

I'm not a roaming catlick
And I sinseerly hope,
That lodes of preying cardigans
Will never make me Pope.

I doan't think I'm a anglian
I'd hayte to wear a hassock,
Or be like Robert Runcie,
And gneel apon a cassock.

I gnow who started metherdists,
John Wesslee did of corse,
But I'm no good at showting
And I cannot ryde a hoarse.

I doont think I'm a batpist,
I even hayte the rain!
When they poosh me in the warter,
Will I come upp againe?

I cood go to a howse church,
But I am reather bad,
At looking very happy,
When I am fealing sad.

Why doon't we start a nue cherch, Pope,
Where evvrything is reel?
I've eeven got a nayme for it-
The cherch of John Paul Veal

Aperson

WINCHESTER CATHEDRAL

I wept in Winchester Cathedral once
It was a winter afternoon
After speaking at a lunch in town
There was an hour to fill before my train was due to leave
Yet again, the beauty of that ancient building
Drew me like a child into its echoing embrace
I knew it would, I have such scant resistance to cathedrals
Particularly this one
This time I did two things
First of all the lighting of a candle for my father
Just because I wanted to
Theology is very thin sometimes
A candle's flame is fat and rich with mystery
The second thing was climbing to the balcony
(They let you do that now)
And, as I stood there, leaning on the rail
Feeling warm at last and looking down
My heart went out to this old, slumberous house of worship
Built for God
Its stonework soaked with centuries of prayer
Tears and passions of belief and doubt
Flowing from a million souls
How can you tolerate these days, I softly asked
The whispering obeisance of the secular patrols?
And then, quite suddenly, the children came
A hundred juniors or more

They sounded like a flock of seagulls
Looked like litter blown in by an enterprising gust of wind
They flung their coats down anywhere, and then
Armed with crayons, paper, pens and question sheets
They looked and listened, wrote and chattered,
    rubbed and roamed
With no respect at all for silly, solemn things
The place was full of them, their virtues and their sins

The building seemed to wake and blink
    and shake itself and smile
And draw itself to its full height with pleasurable pride
On finding all those children working, laughing, living
Unequivocally being there
And that was when I cried
Because I saw, and felt inside, the truth we once received
Long ago, before there were cathedrals
That such as these – these unreligious children
With their earnestness, their busy-ness
Their unselfconscious cries
Form the best of congregations
For they simply are beloved
(Much against the will of serious disciples)
By the only one who ever recognised
Like photographs of home
The Kingdom in their eyes

TOO MUCH DYING

Too much dying don't you think?

Too much screeching metal
Sudden impact
Unexpected endings
Too much mindless murder
Too many killer-dogs
Too many children dying in abandoned freezers
Too many sad, sad rooms
Too many tears
Too much turning finally away
Too much agony of body, mind, memory
Too much grief, melting lives like wax at gravesides
Too many guns
Too much wild, wild callousness
Too little imagination

We can do something, can't we?
We can support political change
We can prohibit the sale of arms
We can send peace-keeping forces
We can deal with social conditions that cause crime
We can put muzzles on dogs
We can put out more publicity about freezers
We can make it harder to pass the driving test

We can find new ways to slow people down
We can teach kids to be as scared of roads
    as they are of strangers.
We can get something going on Breakfast Television
We can do something, can't we?

Yes, but let's not tell people about Jesus
Let's not make it clear that he hates final endings
    as much as we do
Let's not pass on the fact that he has overcome this death
    we dread
Let's not push it down anyone's throat
Even if it is an airway
Let's not offend anyone by mentioning the cross
Or the scream that ripped itself from him
    when the thing was finished
Let's not pass on the news that he came back from the dead
    and lived
Oh, don't tell them that they can do the same
Don't let anyone understand that this tiny corner of eternity
    will pass

Let's not use words like salvation
Redemption
Heaven
Hell
Fire and Brimstone are just symbols – aren't they?
Only fanatics would want folk to avoid
    whatever Jesus died to save us from
Let's assure everybody that all religions are beams of
    light
Shining from different facets of the same crystal
For goodness' sake, let's keep both feet on the ground
Let's be accommodating
Let's be focused
But liberal
Let's compromise
Let's keep the peace
Let's hope, for all our sakes,
    that when the final reckoning is made
We got it right

Too much dying, don't you think?

I WANT TO BE TOUCHED

I want to be touched by affectionate eyes,
I want to be welcomed when welcome is rare,
I want to be held when my confidence sighs,
I want to find comfort in genuine care

I want to be given untakeable things,
I want to be trusted with hearts that might break,
I want to fly dreaming on effortless wings,
I want to be smiled on when I awake.

I want to see sunsets with people I know,
I want to hear secrets that no-one should hear,
I want to be guarded wherever I go,
I want to be fought for when dangers appear.

I want to be chained to the lives of my friends,
I want to be wanted because and despite,
I want to link arms when the foolishness ends,
I want to be safe in the merciless night.

I want to be sheltered although I am wrong,
I want to be laughed at although I am right,
I want to be sung in the heavenly song,
I want to be loved, I want to be light.

FREELY I CONFESS

Freely I confess my sins
For God has poured his grace in
But when another lists my faults
I want to smash his face in

NIGHT TALK (1 KINGS 9:1-2)

You really did appear to him at night?
In what form did you come to him at night?
Were you an angel entertained awares?
Or just a 'really feel the Lord is saying'
Half a thought, halfway up the stairs
Pure sensation buoying up his heart
Inhabiting his prayers
Perhaps a line of Scripture meaning something special
Shining for a day?
If so, well, that's okay . . .
But – were you just a dream, so real, but just a dream?
A natural way of saying
All I ever said I stand by still
Or – listen – did you stand or kneel beside his bed
And reach out with your hand
To softly touch his head?
No awesome fire, no glory too great to behold
But something like his father, only more so
Comfort in the waking, in the meeting of the eyes
Was he amazed to see you
And to sense the passion beating
In a heart that only yesterday
With overwhelming light
Had filled the temple?

COSIER THAN COTTAGES

Cosier than cottages are warm cathedrals filled with faith,
But rather grant that they should fall, Oh Lord,
Than let such glories stand preserved as cold, majestic barns,
Where crates of Christianity are darkly, dumbly stored

CONFESSING

My conscience is clear about Gandhi's career,
I didn't impede him one jot,
I've never set lions on free-church Hawaiians
(I've wanted to do so a lot).
Nor am I the type to knock out my pipe,
On a twenty-stone Sumo for fun,
And despite all that mess in the *Daily Express*,
I've never played chess on a nun.
I fight all temptations to napalm small nations,
It's just as old-fashioned a scheme,
As feeding your Panda with maps of Uganda,
However astute that may seem.
I've never bombed Yale nor harpooned a whale,
Nor flirted with visiting popes,
I fiercely resist being lustfully kissed,
By the stars of American soaps.
I'm well in accord with the words of Our Lord,
Where he tells us just how we should pray,
He tells us prayer strength isn't measured in length,
So I pray for three seconds a day.
I know God won't bless any tithing unless,
We can cheerfully give, and not fret,
As I don't find it funny to part with my money,
I've not given anything yet.
I ought to feel great in my virtuous state,
Uniquely, a moral success,
So why do I sense there is something immense
That I urgently need to confess?

WORDS FROM THE CROSS

I

FATHER FORGIVE THEM,
THEY KNOW NOT WHAT THEY DO

Some insisted that the journey
Was a waste of hope and time
Better to embrace the darkness
Set apart for such a crime
Still they travelled onward, upward
Stumbled, staggered, rose and fell
Just to own one glimpse of heaven
In the sightless pits of Hell
At the gates the angels waited
Menace burned in every eye
Then the ranks abruptly parted
As there rose a joyful cry
'Let them pass, these weary travellers
Every one my blood defends
Bring the best that Heaven offers,
These who killed me are my friends'

II
TODAY YOU WILL BE WITH ME IN PARADISE

I begged you to remember me,
But feared that you might say,
'It all depends on how your prayer-life grows,
As everybody knows, you cannot go to Heaven
If your quiet-time is short,
And have you let a wicked thought
Pass through your wicked mind today?
I trust you fought it all the way, and won.
A word about your worship – is it from the heart?
Do you take part with lifted arms,
And loudly echo "Hallelujah!"
When the pastor socks it to yer?
Do you think predestination
Is the stop before your station?
Such a weak apology for genuine theology,
Will never gain you access to the place where I must go.'
You might have said those fearful things, oh, Lord,
My heart was faint within me, I confess
But when I said 'Will you remember me?'
You simply smiled and softly answered, 'Yes'

III

WOMAN BEHOLD YOUR SON

Today I do not want to be a branch of the vine
Or a part of the body
Or a sheep in the flock of the Good Shepherd
Or the bride of Christ
Or a disciple
Or a servant
Or an inheritor of the Kingdom
Or a citizen of Heaven
Or visited by angels
Or greatly blessed
Or deeply troubled
Or someone else's mother
I just want to get my son down from this wooden thing
And take him home
And make him better
And give him something to eat
And hear him laugh
And persuade him to give up being the Messiah
And go back to carpentry

IV

MY GOD, MY GOD,
WHY HAVE YOU FORSAKEN ME?

On this particular day, I feel a failure
What am I allowed to wonder, Father
Am I allowed to wonder why you make it all so difficult?
Even as I say those words the guilt settles.
Perhaps it isn't really difficult at all.
Probably it's me that's difficult.
Probably, because of my background,
    and my temperament,
and my circumstances,
    it was always going to be difficult for me.
But what if that's just a cop-out?
What if I'm kidding myself?
What if, deep inside, I know that my own deliberate doing
and not doing has always made it difficult?
What if I'm one of those who has been called,
    but not chosen?
In that case it's not difficult – it's impossible.
What if you don't exist at all,
    and death is a sudden stumble into silence?
(Can you let me know if you don't exist, by the way –
 before Friday night, if it's all the same to you?)
There are moments, Father, when it's so easy,
So easy that I can't remember
    why it ever seemed so difficult.

Those moments pass – they're valuable – but they pass.
Have you noticed how, when those moments have gone,
I try to walk away, but I can't?
I think I shall follow you even if you don't exist.
Even if I'm not chosen.
Even if it goes on being difficult . . .
Are you still listening?
I'm sorry to have made such a fuss,
It's just that, on this particular day, I feel a failure.
My feet and my hands hurt,
And there's this pain in my side.

V

I THIRST

Today I wept for all my trying
Hurrying to meet the children out of school
I spilled my dreams upon the kitchen floor
And couldn't stop to mop them at the time
No doubt they'll dry and bear the marks of careless feet.
Returning, I had barely closed the door
Before I knew I must return to town
They had no drinks
And if I failed to provide
The Coke, the squash, the lemonade
I knew I would be roundly cursed
Dear Lord, while others drink until they're satisfied
Remember me
I thirst

VI
IT IS FINISHED

It is finished
Finished?
Is it?
I don't think so
Not until the funny little woman on the Friday bus
Means more to me than I do to myself
Not until I read aright the message of your pain-filled eyes
That I must take the ones you loved and left behind
To live with me as my responsibility
Not until I freely place my stock of cherished certainties
Like sad surrendered weapons at your injured feet
Not until the public and the private faces
of my troubled Christianity
Can meet, and know they recognised each other
when they met
Not until I know the names
of more than half the people in my street
Finished?
Is it?
No, I don't think so
Not yet

VII
FATHER, INTO YOUR HANDS
I COMMIT MY SPIRIT

How is it possible to be so many things?
Success and failure sit within my life
   like children on a double swing
One takes me high and then the other
Once I dreamed of swinging high enough
   to see the tops of tallest towers
But I have had enough of swinging now
I want to take the swing down from the bough
And sit out on the lawn and watch the flowers
I would settle happily for peaceful sunshine days
A little gentle praise
A smile that passes softly now and then
   between the two of us
A single glance that knows and understands
Can something of this nature be arranged?
Father, grant me sense and strength enough
   to place my spirit in your hands
Or I must swing until a chain breaks
No more failure, no success, no swings
And me a broken victim of these unimportant things

THE DOWNS

Why do I love the Downs?
Because they crunch and rattle
Beneath us as we walk
Brittle bones of flint
Yielding flesh of chalk
Because the sun's unpanicked here, and free
Dawdles on a hilltop
Skips around a bit
Paints a dream of heaven
Gossips kindly with a stunted tree

Why do I love the Downs?
Because they prove
That valleys can't climb hills
That spirit sometimes rests
When body wills
They've never let us down, the Downs
They raise our kites
Raise our children
Higher, better than we ever could
Down here in temporary television towns

WE SAW THE STEAM TRAINS FLY

From Tunbridge Wells to Eridge,
    Heathfield, Horam, Hellingly,
Through Hailsham, Polegate, Hampden Park,
    we saw the steam trains fly.
One long remembered seaside day,
    before the clock strikes six,
As morning pours out sunshine
    on our pavement made of bricks,
We run with picnic, towels and trunks
    (and macs in case of rain)
To meet the bus that takes us down
    to meet the Eastbourne train.
How smashing – how fantastic to get off at Tunbridge Wells,
To hurry to the old West Station sniffing steam train smells.
To board the sooty monster that will thunder down the line,
To where the screaming seagulls dive
    towards the froth and shine.
The journey starts and soon we stop at tiny Eridge Station,
Eridge people pile in to share our destination.
John is first to get told off: 'If you make nasty smells,
We're getting off at Heathfield,
    there's a bus to Tunbridge Wells!'
Heathfield comes and Heathfield goes, John is smelly good,
We won't be going home by bus,
    we never thought we would.
Are we nearly there yet? all the children ask,
Can we have a sandwich now?

– I'm thirsty, where's the flask?
I hope you brought my bucket
    – did you bring it? Are you sure?
Mum, I'm bored – I want the toilet – *why* can't I explore?
Is this Eastbourne? No, it's Horam.
    Ian's got sweets, it isn't fair,
If you saved money you'd have sweets.
    Mum, are we *nearly* there?
Two men get off at Hellingly, a mystery to me,
What's the point of getting off before you reach the sea?
In and out of Hailsham, past fields of cows and sheep,
Ian is lost in comics, John is fast asleep,
But as we puff to Polegate I am sure I smell the sea,
And hear the crash of breaking waves as clearly as can be.
Oh, to live in Hampden Park,
    with Eastbourne just next door,
To walk or cycle every day in minutes to the shore!
The engine pants and hisses,
    brakes are shrieking, squealing loud,
John wakes, we gather up our things
    and join the Eastbourne crowd.
From Tunbridge Wells to Eridge,
    Heathfield, Horam, Hellingly,
Through Hailsham, Polegate, Hampden Park,
    we saw the steam trains fly.

UNDISTINGUISHED CORNERS

Lets play (improvised) instruments (badly) to celebrate the
   reclamation of damaged things that have cluttered the
   backyard in undistinguished corners for years, and ought
   to have been got rid of some time ago.
Let us stick our fingers on the end of bicycle pumps to make
   squeaky noises
Clink milk bottles together
Make Australian sounds with a sheet of hardboard
Pluck the prongs of a fork
Jingle the change in our pockets
Squeeze the palms of our hands squelchily together
Blow paper bags up and burst them with a bang
Let the air out of a balloon so that it sounds like a violin
Bounce gently on a stair that creaks
Push a stiff brush across the linoleum
Flicker the pages of a book
Blow screeching noises through blades of grass held
   between our thumbs
And drum frenziedly with toothpicks on cushions
For he became man and dwelt among us
And we beheld his glory in the back yard
And, for some strange reason, he enjoys our music.

THE AGONY OF PAINLESSNESS

The black rain that falls
Into a river of blood
Is swept to the bowels of the earth
As white-hot evil mud
This, for me, is joy

The angry sun explodes
Shards of searing heat
Shower the cringing human race
Slicing flesh like butcher's meat
This, for me, is gentleness

The boiling sea overflows
Dry land melts and screams
Congealing into twisted shapes
Fetid ghouls in hellish dreams
This, for me, is peace

The sobbing of the universe
Essence of primeval pain
Echoes through the bludgeoned skulls
Of orphans crushed and crudely slain
This, for me, is care

MOTHER

I remember when my father said
'You'll drive your mother mad if you're not good'
That night I dreamed I had
I saw her sitting on a chair in some sad cell
Nodding, grinning, knowing no-one, driven mad indeed
Lost forever to the wicked child who turned her mind
By being bad
The horror woke me
In the dark my thoughts were white and scraped and raw
I had to call her in to sit beside me looking safely sane
I silently resolved I would be good for ever more
And was – all night.

I remember when I learned at school
Just how the hornbeam leaf
   can be distinguished from the elm
I told my mother
'With the hornbeam,
   one side starts a little further down, you see'
She seemed to be so fascinated
Said how she would need to see this for herself
Next day, although a crashing, blowing,
   soaking storm had broken out
I ran into the woods when school had ended
Searching frenziedly for hornbeam trees and elms
As the weather beat me up I may have cried
But there was so much wet about

I only know I streamed with it and didn't care.
How excited she would be to see it for herself
The way in which the hornbeam
    is distinguished from the elm
When I got home I'd caught a chill and had to go to bed
But downstairs in the lounge my trophy twigs
    stood proudly in a vase
And stayed there long beyond the time
    when they were dead.

And I remember all those nights
When I, a pasty teenage renegade
Came creeping home way past the fury hour
No sound, no lights,
    no comfort for an unrepentant prodigal like me
Except that when I reached out gently in the dark
I'd find a little pile of marmite sandwiches
And touch the chilly smoothness of a glass of milk
My mother put them there because the life of God in her
Gave gifts with all the passion of a punishment
To those she loved beyond reproach
Marmite and milk still comfort me.

And I remember all the pain my mother felt
Through years of staring at a mirror telling vicious lies
About the optimistic child in her
So sad
That so much happiness was spilled and wasted
Drained and lost
Until at last the mirror cracked, and, being on her own
She suddenly remembered who she was
Though God and me – we'd always known.

CLOTHES

Clothes maketh the man
Who dressed you this morning, Man?
Who stuck that skin-tight skin
   on those poorly chosen bones?
Only bones you've got I guess
Some say that's all we are
Skin and bone
Even the fat ones – especially the fat ones
I say
We say
He says
Never mind skin and bone
Check your treasure
Check it's safe.

PLAYGROUND

Oh, God, I'm not anxious to snuff it,
But when the grim reaper reaps me – and me,
We'll try to rely on our vision of Zion,
We know how we want it to be.
As soon as you greet us in Heaven,
And ask what we'd like, we shall say,
'We just want a chance for our spirits to dance,
We want to be able to play.'

Tell the angels to build a soft playground,
Designed and equipped just for me – and me,
With a vertical slide that's abnormally wide,
And oceans of green PVC.
There'll be reinforced netting to climb on,
And rubberised floors that will bend,
And no-one can die, so we needn't be shy,
If we're tempted to land on a friend.

We'll go mad in the soft, squashy mangle,
And barmy with balls in the swamp,
Coloured and spherical – we'll be hysterical,
We'll have a heavenly romp.
There'll be cushions and punchbags and tyres,
In purple and yellow and red,
And a mushroomy thing that will suddenly sing,
When we kick it or sit on its head.

There'll be fountains of squash and Ribena,
To feed our continual thirst,
And none of that stuff about, 'You've had enough',
Surely heavenly bladders won't burst.
We might be too tall for the entrance,
But Lord, throw the rules in the bin,
If we are too large, tell the angel in charge,
To let us bow down and come in.

I CANNOT MAKE YOU LOVE ME

If I wanted I could take the light
One shining sheet of paper
Crush it in my fist
And then – it would be night
If I was so inclined
I could destroy the day with fire
Warm my hands at all your charred tomorrows
With the smallest movement of my arm
One flicker of my will
Sweep you and all your darkness from the land
But I cannot make you love me
Cannot make you love me
I cannot make you, will not make you,
Cannot make you love me

If I wanted I could lift the sea
As if it were a turquoise tablecloth
Uncover lost forgotten things
Unwritten history
It would be easy to revive the bones
Of men who never thought to see their homes again
I have revived one shipwrecked man in such a way
The story of that rescuing, that coming home
Might prove I care for you
But though I can inscribe I LOVE YOU in the sky
    and on the sea
I cannot make you love me

I cannot make you, will not make you,
Cannot make you love me

I can be Father, Brother, Shepherd, Friend
The Rock, the Door, the Light, Creator, Son of Man
Emmanuel, Redeemer, Spirit, First and Last,
    the Lion or the Lamb
I can be Master, Lord, the Way, the Truth, the Wine
Bread or Bridegroom, Son of God, I am, Jehovah
Saviour, Judge, the Cornerstone, the Vine
I can be King of Kings, Deliverer, the Morning Star
Alpha, Omega, Jesus, Rabbi,
    Carpenter or Morning Dew
Servant, Teacher, Sacrifice, the Rose of Sharon
I can be – I have been – crucified for you
But I cannot make you love me
Cannot make you love me
I cannot make you, will not make you,
Cannot make you love me

Silences and Nonsenses

SECRET FRIENDS

Throughout our nearly forty years together my wife Bridget and I have been privileged to meet quite a lot of the secret friends of God, people who follow Jesus and serve others without acquiring power that manages to disguise itself as humility, or by inventing a new branch of theology, or a fresh move of the Spirit. We love to encounter these quiet heroes. Their lives are reassuring, their example profoundly inspiring. In the first five years of the new century we were fortunate enough to be invited to make two trips abroad on behalf of the aid agency World Vision, one to Bangladesh and the other to Zambia. For the first time we were able to witness the work being done by unassuming servants of God in parts of the world where the degree of poverty and sickness offers challenges that are unimaginable in this country.

We were certainly excited by the prospect of these adventures, but we also felt woefully inadequate. *Poverty* was written very shortly after our arrival in Dhaka. I was horrified, less by the impenetrable forest of poverty and suffering that we witnessed than by my reaction to it. *Bangladeshi Baby* embodies a kind of solution to this obsession with my personal inadequacies. We do the thing that we are given to do and, as the last line of the poem tries to say, the rest of it is no business of ours. What is certain is that we returned home with an even deeper respect for those who unselfishly ensure that Jesus still walks the streets of these centres of deprivation. The phrase *Secret Friends* is taken from *Image of the Invisible God*, one of the poems in this section.

What of me? was inspired by Bishop Tom Wright's challenging contention that if we do not believe Jesus doubted his own divinity we have not begun to understand the New Testament. *And Jesus will be Born* is rooted in a growing conviction that, no matter how dark and difficult a situation may be, the pattern of incarnation, death and resurrection will always be available in one form or another. This poem means a great deal to me, but as yet I cannot hit on the best way to deliver it. I shall go on trying . . .

2000–2005

WITH THE REST

MARY REMEMBERS

Those real-life, legendary, famous men
Who ate the Sabbath corn with him
a thousand puzzled memories ago
Are far more confident today
They play their humble trumpets in the market place
Clarion the truth
How Jesus was and is the image of his Father
Full of love and grace and truth
And yes, of course he was and is his Father's son
The Holy one, the Saviour
Yes, of course he was
Of course he is
And yet, you know, that baby, once so closely mine
That baby who became a boy, a man, and much, much more
Inherited from me the things my mother's heart loved best
His nose, his ears
That way he had of lifting up his chin
when the road was getting rough
Such special joy to see these sweet,
sweet things all risen with the rest
Not much perhaps, but privately, for me – enough

WHAT OF ME?

Yes, he will rise again
But what of me?
Though death flaps down to take me like a huge black bird
Casting ragged shadows over lilies of the valley
Over milky moonlit seas
Sunrise glory
Sunset flame
Peach and pearl in Galilean skies
The coolness of a woman's hand
Children's eyes
The rasp of rough-grained wood against the skin
Light in the gaze of men, who,
    by a miracle of faith, have seen
Heard, walked, talked
Discovered that their pitted skin is whole and clean
Sabbath walks, meandering through rolling fields of wheat
The chattering and chuckling of my friends
Their sweet naivety
A scent of cooking fish
The call to eat
Old stories by the fire
Good wine
A kiss

Love and wisdom in my mother's smile
The tears of those who loved me much
Because I gently, fiercely took away their sin
And will I rise again?
Indeed, the son of man must rise and live once more
But what of me?
What of me?

CRAZY GOLF

There is not much more
Need not be more
Than playing Crazy Golf in France
Laughing in the summer rain

TO BE A PILGRIM

He who would valiant be, let him come hither
Well, yes, quite
Absolutely – let him come!
I'll be along in a minute
Not that I'm against hithering, you understand
I'm a hitherer
I am a hithering person – definitely am a potential one
It's just that – well,
    I've had to put the old hithering on hold for a bit
I suppose you could say I'm in the Slough of thing
Thingy
Things
The Slough of things
That man was right
    – couple of friendly bombs probably do the trick
Hmmm . . .
First avowed intent still intact, mind you
Oh, yes, to be – a proper one
To be a pilgrim
The thing is, modern pilgrimming doesn't quite hit the . . .
Err – well, you know,
    the jolly old sort of churchy High thingy thing
Day off
Smart casual gear
Hope it doesn't rain
Who're you walking with?
Very profound experience

Has a very special meaning for me
Flowers are wonderful
Go every year
Usually get a coach together
Very good talk
Smashing meal
Charming little bed and breakfast.
Tidy prayers
Been happening for hundreds of years
That and the effort of the walking seems to add depth to it
Sort of thing
Nothing wrong with all that, of course
Nothing wrong
Very right
But . . .
Pilgrimming
Pilgrimming for me

Can we afford?
Did I remember?
I should have done it then
Oh, not again
All right, I'm sorry – I'm sorry – I'm sorry!
It didn't mean anything, honestly
I promise I won't
I promise I will
I promise I'll promise to promise that I'll promise anything
Someone at the door . . .

Why the hell should I?
Why the hell shouldn't I?
Yes, of course I will – you know I will
Ow! Ow! My leg! Ow!
　　Hurts too much to go on a pilgrimage . . .
Sort of thing
Beset me round with dismal stories?
Dismal, abysmal – oh, yes! Oh, yes! Oh, yes!
My strength the more is?
No-o-o-o, no, no, no!
Well, look, never mind
　　– we know we at the end shall life inherit
At least, we shall if –
Tell me, do your fancies seem to flee away?
Mine don't
Large, lazy, flightless birds, my fancies,
　　like one-legged emus
They just lurch around and around and around in circles . . .
Do you know, I really rather fear what men say
I suppose
The long and the short of it is
　　– I do labour night and day – in a way
But
I'm not sure I've even begun
To be a pilgrim

WINTER WAKING

Winter waking, stretched across the moonstone sky
Caring less than nothing for the destiny of man
You see the crows, like ragged scraps of dustbin bag
Come floating down the wind
To scavenge what they can
And nothing need be spoken
Deep in winter sleep is where you hear the saddest cry
The wheeling dealing seagull souls
Of men and women taught to stay a step ahead
Who reached the edge
But found that when they fell
They had not learned to fly
I tell you that it drives you wild
It drives you out to march and march
beside the heartless sea
To weep and rage
And beg the only one who really knows
To tell you, tell you, tell you, tell you why
So many hearts are broken

WHEN YOU SLEPT

When you slept, on the cushion, in the boat
Did you dream the walk we took
You and I
One autumn afternoon
From that little church at Lullington
Through Littlington to Alfriston
Where ageless fields of flint and chalk
Fell seamlessly to merge and meet
With green and violet shadows
That were circling and embracing
The cathedral of the Downs?
I was in terror of a storm that day
The red and gold flew and fluttered round our heads
Brittle messages of loss and pain and death
The surging valley-side beyond us
Once a way to rise
I suddenly discerned
Was nothing but a dumb and loveless wall
Sad to see familiar beauty now a thing of ugliness,
   I dropped my gaze
You spoke a word
A firm command
Into the centre of the raging storm
And when at last I raised my eyes
I saw with grateful wonder
That the splendour had returned

POVERTY

On arrival in Dhaka – Bangladesh

Poverty comes tapping on the windows of our car
But I know the ropes
Stay quite calm, don't meet their eyes
Relationship is fatal
Register no silent questions
Offer no replies
For God's sake don't explain
Don't say
Now look, you haven't understood
I'm on your side
I'm sponsored by World Vision
An international agency
I'm here to write a book for them, here to help the poor
The profits will all go to you
Well, no, not you precisely, but to people just like you
Well, slightly younger and –
Look, just stop tapping on the window, will you?
Go away – I've told you that I care about the poor
We all do, every one of us inside this car
No, no, no, it's really not as simple as the needs
you have today

You – you have to go and be where there's a project
That's the way it works – it has to be like that, you see
It's got to be well organised
These one-off payments never work, because –
Get off my window
Have you taken in a single word I've said?
It's not about your current need to eat
Try to understand
The key word is community
Social change will trickle down and help the individual to . . .
Please take your hollow eyes
    and outstretched hand away from me
I do not want you
You are frighteningly thin
You make me feel so bad
When poverty came tapping at the window of our car
I knew the ropes

BANGLADESHI BABY

Little baby Bangladesh
Bursting with your Bangla, Belgian, British, Bantu babiness
You flatter me
You babies always do
By nestling to my chest
And in your eyes, Bangla baby,
   in those dark and dusky pools,
I see that you know all you need to know for now
And we who think we know much more are fools
For sadly all our wisdom offers for your future
Is much less than you will need
Little baby Bangladesh
Clutching at my collar with your tiny boxing Bangla fists
Please let me say a prayer for you
A supplication on your infant head
I hope your baby legs grow strong
Walk well upon these dusty streets
And find each day your daily bread
God grant a love that fills your heart, a life that will be long
May you be loved, and blessed with friends,
   and often kissed, and free
And Bangla baby that will be enough
I do not ask that you remember me

IMAGE OF THE INVISIBLE GOD

Image of the invisible God
Given for us
A lover of nature
Committed
Aggressive
Accessible
Uncompromising
Strangely meek
A story teller
Master of timing
Hardworking
Relaxed
Emotional
Passionate
Compassionate
Prayerful
A radical
A wit
A good son
A good friend
An enjoyer of parties
He relished the company of people
But did not trust the hearts of men
Filled with sadness
Filled with joy
Filled with love
Filled with frustration

He adored children because they reminded him of home

Broke his own rules

Angry with enemies and disciples

Happy to get down on his knees to wash feet

A man with secret friends

Needy

Troubled

Terrified

Obedient

Lost

Lonely

Neglected

Very badly hurt

Courageous

Unpredictable

Dead

Alive

Triumphant

Forgiving

A lover of the lost

A man who knew how to cook fish

Given for us

Image of the invisible God

NO AGENDA

I offer you my heart and soul,
My money and my life,
Just don't ever ask me
To say sorry to my wife.

STATISTICS OF DEATH

You are more likely to die travelling by train than by plane
More likely to die in the winter than in the spring
More likely to die in a car-crash than from cancer
More likely to die watching *EastEnders* than *The Weakest Link*
More likely to be murdered than to win the lottery
More likely to die in China than in Spain

You are more likely to die if you starve than if you eat
More likely to die at Old Trafford
    than in an ice-cream parlour
More likely to die in the morning than in the afternoon
More likely to die in Luton than in Milton Keynes
More likely to die in a Polish sentry-box
    than a Morris 1000 Traveller
More likely to die of cold than of heat

You are more likely to die in blue than in green
More likely to die in bed than in Birmingham
More likely to die intestate than on a tandem
More likely to die in company than alone
More likely to die on a Monday than on a Friday
More likely to die where you are than where you have been

You are more likely to die if you are tall than if you are short
More likely to die of hate than of love
More likely to die choking on a marble
　　than to spontaneously combust
More likely to die facing south than facing east
More likely to die on land than on sea
More likely to die from leisure than from sport

You are more likely to die doing the twist than the jive
More likely to die at home than in any other place
More likely to die with friends than with strangers
More likely to die with an apology than with a blessing
More likely to die with a question than an answer
You are *most* likely to die if you are alive

AND JESUS WILL BE BORN

On Christmas day the world will turn once more
towards its end
But Jesus will be born
A woman who has tried once more in vain
to re-create the morning
Will find her spirit crushed at last by failures and defeats
Her grief will trail like tattered ribbons
Through apocalyptic streets
And Jesus will be born

A little child who cannot waste his tiny reservoir of moisture
On a thing as purely pointless as a tear
Will puzzle at the burning skies
Blank and empty as his mother's eyes
And wish beyond the point of fear
That darkness would descend
And Jesus will be born

And in some cold, sad cell
a man will dream of blessed ordinariness
A walk, a meal, a smile, a book, the chance to feel
A trusting hand in his
Small and soft and folded like a flower in the night
Devastating innocence that promises redemption
and has never lied

But will not save him from the morning and the hour
When heavy boots come marching
down the corridor outside
And Jesus will be born

And in a hollow church a hollow priest
Dry and dusty as some jewelled chalice
locked away for safety and for ever
Will sit and sigh and gather oddments, scraps of truth
Remnants of an old, forgotten dream
Ideas and words like autumn leaves
made brittle by a year of death
And by the scorching summer sun
And feel once more so glad, and oh, so very, very sad
That those who delicately brush his sprinkled fragments
from their Sunday-best
Will never hear the distant, panic-stricken scream
And Jesus will be born

At the corner of the street the image of the living God
Will hug herself against the cold
And smoke a friendly cigarette
And be prepared to greet success with weary resignation
Feebly lit by one of yesterday's recycled smiles
And struggle to forget what she was told
When someone was in charge and choices could be made
And there was hope
And Jesus will be born

Yes, Jesus will be born
Though the night enfolds like a black shroud
And the liar's lies drive us from our peace
And take us from our beds
And bring us to our knees
On the cold stone tiles of the kitchen floor
Jesus will be born
Yes, though the skies crack
And the heavens sway
And the heat dies in the earth's core
And the last stitch in the last ditch appears
When all is lost
A child's hand will reach out from the manger
A wounded hand will catch our tears
For Jesus will be born for evermore on Christmas day

Silences and Nonsenses

2005 –2010

INCENSE OF THE HEART

Incense of the Heart is a phrase from *Communion of Lights*, a poem written after our trip to Peru and Bolivia with the wonderful streetchild charity Toybox early in 2008. It describes laughter, a phenomenon that has been a part of my professional life since the first *Sacred Diary* came out in 1987. Apart from anything else I am a serial spoofer. I know few pleasures greater than parodying some po-faced collection of words. How sad is that? *Elbows and Ephods* is a reaction to memories of choruses that made little sense to my untutored teenage brain. They seemed to consist of a solid wodge of words lifted whole from some obscure Old Testament book, involving terminology that appeared impenetrable. Maybe we sing too many things without asking ourselves what they really mean – if anything.

The serious side of laughter is its therapeutic and releasing function. It relaxes and reassures and sometimes provides a little holiday in the Monday morning endlessness of grief. Over the last few years Bridget and I have seen wonderful things happening when people simply laugh. Of course, not everyone agrees that laughter is 'of God'. They want to know where it is mentioned in Scripture. In a recent Bible note Bridget commented on these doubts.

'Of course the Bible is vital for spiritual growth, but God has also provided clues in the rest of his creation as to how he wants us to be. Take babies, for example. A small baby's gurgling chuckle has to be one of the most wonderful sounds in the world. A sense of fun is built into our design . . .'

A Little Girl Picks up a Stick by High Force Waterfall and *Someone I knew* are verbal snapshots, records of tiny, ordinary moments that were intensely significant when they happened. I have begun to understand the profound importance of small, important events in people's lives. A phrase, a look, a sunset, a hand slipped into yours, a kindness, shared tears, laughter over silly things, a walk in the rain, these are the mystical experiences that make change and progress possible. They are not in the Bible, and they are all in the Bible.

Once I Walked with You and *When in Doubt* make similar points. Spiritual navel-gazing is probably a waste of time. So much needs doing in this world, and sharing out the Grace of God has the same effect as using your hot-water tank. It gets filled up again. It seems very fitting to me that the last words in the last bit of verse in this book sum up this call to obedience: *Just do it.*

IF I WAS GOD
I WOULDN'T LET THE CHILDREN DIE

If I was God I wouldn't let the children die
Not me, I'd use my power
Wouldn't you?
You'd never find me sitting round in heaven
Twiddling my eternal thumbs
As some poor baby fades to nothing
Wailing for a love that never comes

I'd get my act together, heal some pain
Hurl some thunder
Send some rain
Clothe some orphans
Dig some wells
Throw some parties
Ring some bells
Feed some kids
Win some fights
Build some homes
Fly some kites
That's what I would do

I'd look for helpers who would be my hands and feet
They'd show my face in every slum and street
They'd broadcast love and let compassion fly
That's what I would do if I was God
I wouldn't let the children die
Would you?

A LITTLE GIRL PICKS UP A STICK
ON THE PATH DOWN TO
HIGH FORCE WATERFALL IN CUMBRIA

At first she thought it might be something good to eat
But found it slightly sharp when she touched it to her lips
Perhaps a pencil, hold it like a pencil
No, no point
No point
A thing you wave towards the sky?
Yes!
Fallen from a tree
A thing that waves towards the sky
Glance at some internal clock
Quick! Time to skip
Dropped the stick forever
On to see the waterfall, whatever that might be
On the path the stick lay still and stick-like
Totally fulfilled

SOMEONE I KNEW

I was sitting in a café on my own
Someone I knew walked past the window
Someone I knew!
There!
Just walking past the window
Someone I knew and who knew me
Walking past the plate-glass window!
So – how to handle it
I worried that if I left my place the waiter would not
understand
He might remove my coffee and my garlic bread
He might think that I had left
I went anyway
Tried to signal that I would be back
I doubt he understood or noticed
I hurried out and caught the person that I knew
I said hello, so did he, then he walked on
It was just someone I knew

WHAT IS GOD?

He's an angel, he's a book
He's the moon, he's the sun
He's a baby; he's a pillar of fire.

He's a guide, he's a priest
He's a chicken, he's a rose
He's the leader of a heavenly choir.

He's a father, he's a son
He's a brother, he's a spirit
He's a horseman, he's a prophet
He's a preacher.

He's a friend, he's a shield
He's a star, he's a saviour
He's a walker on the water
He's a teacher.

He's a shepherd, he's a vine
He's a mighty rushing wind
He's a rabbi, he's a healer
He's a door,

He's a cloud, he's a builder
He's a giant clap of thunder
He's a lion with a deafening roar.

He's a dancer, he's a cook
He's a word, he's a lamb
He's a dove
He's an eagle on the wing.

He's a ruler, he's a refuge
He's a lover, he's a light
He's a bridegroom
He's a servant, he's a king.

LEWIS AND FRIENDS

Tolkien on the toilet
Dyson in the bath
Williams does the washing up
Lewis sweeps the hearth
Not an inkling, not a clue
That future generations
Would passionately long to share
These humble occupations

DAYS OF MY LIFE

The sun
The moon
The stars
Hung high in heaven for my delight
Mysterious gifts
A mobile that will draw my hands
My eyes, my life
Will teach me shape and fill my heart with wonder
   and with smiling

There is not space
In this round world
To fling my hands
My heart my body
They are rockets
I will fire them to the edges of the universe
To circle and to race the flying planets
In the star-bedazzled cosmos of my spirit

One road only now
It must not be the one that I have travelled
I try, I tried, but walls rise up
And strong, unyielding voices tell me
Onward is the way, you may not stand
The broad and narrow paths,
   all choice has vanished with the days
One road only now

I sometimes fear what I may find
Always in the past
Autumn was the richest time
But now I stumble in the fallen leaves
My body and my heart are frail
I have mislaid the magic
And imagination's power
Warm confidence that winter's coldest, darkest hour
Contains within its heart the hidden fire of spring

HOLES IN YOUR LIFE

When you fall through the holes in your life
Don't think it surprising or odd
Be glad that it's planned you will finally land
On the solid forgiveness of God

ELBOWS AND EPHODS

We raise our elbows to the ephod in the sanctuary,
We cleanse our gourds from water pots
    that once were sealed,
We gather at the sacred stones of Zebulon
Where the sons of Eli's nephews will be healed.

And they who once were not will not be not now,
And they who were will now no longer be,
And they who thought they were
    will now know that they are not,
And the whole thing will remain a mystery.

And I must go and feed my kangaroo now,
He's juggling Lego on the kitchen range
He's changed his name from Albert to Virginia,
I think I need a week at Ellel Grange

DAMN! I WISH I'D PRAYED

I drove to town this morning, it wasn't very far,
But all the way I asked myself where I would park the car.
Imagine my amazement when, in Devonshire Parade,
I found a perfect parking space!
Damn! I wish I'd prayed.

In April at Spring Harvest our chalet was complete,
Except that towels were not supplied,
   we'd have to use a sheet.
My chalet-mate said,
   'Problem solved, my son's come to our aid,
His car was stacked with extra towels!'
Damn! I wished we'd prayed.

We planned a parish picnic on a day in late July,
Hoping that in summertime the weather would be dry.
When I awoke to cloudy skies and rain I was dismayed,
But just in time the sun came out!
Damn! I wish I'd prayed.

Long ago in Eden Eve and Adam broke the law,
When they consumed those apples
   I was doomed for evermore,
But Jesus came to earth, and through the sacrifice he made,
I've found a way back home to God!
Damn! I wish I'd prayed.

SISTER

You cannot join the cavalcade
Nor take my hand at celebration fires
Though, in the place where people meet and eat
Your grace will grace me still
A place will not be laid
And if I cannot catch your sweetly singing eye
Across the tuneless choirs
How shall I stem the weeping of the secretly betrayed
This child in me who hardly ever dared to speak a word,
And never will do now, for fear of being heard?

HUNGRY RICH MEN

Hungry rich men hunger for me
Would, if they were able, pour me
Into gaping fathomless abysses
Long to feast upon the kisses
Of my sweet, inestimable poverty
See them coming with their camels
Laden high with all they have admired
Nothing that they bring will ease their famine
Nor will they believe the gateway to my storehouse
   is so very, very small
Not ever, not at all
They did not truly know until today what they desired

THE HEAD CAME IN BY HELICOPTER

After meeting street children in Cochabamba,
Bolivia, 2009

The head came in by helicopter
Not the body
That came up in trucks
The body of the Christ was far too big
To haul up all at once
And they had to haul it up
To get the damn thing there
To build the white monstrosity
With Ayatollah eyes
And not a trace of kindness in its face
Nor any human warmth
In that symmetrical embrace
They had to built it on the summit
Visible, but coldly uninvolved
With all the messy stuff
That happens at the bottom of the hill
Nothing given, nothing sacrificed
We climbed a thousand steps inside the hollow statue
Spiralled up towards the helicoptered head
And found that we were noticing
A nasty smell of urine in the body of the Christ

Far, far below the dead thing on the hill
The risen Lord of all creation
Ten years old and reeling from the damage to his head
Cradled someone's filthy infant in his arms
And looking up for just an instant
From the Square of San Sebastian
Saw that figure shining on the hill
Shook his head in puzzlement
Gently stroked his baby's head, and said
'Who is that man?'

192

COMMUNION OF LIGHTS
An evening spent with pastors
and street workers in Bolivia

We couldn't hold a candle to those people
But we did exactly that
One night in dark Oruru where the devil steals
   the name of God
And followers of Jesus battle day and night
To save the light that can so quickly die in children's eyes
We asked for darkness so that each of us
Could light a candle from our neighbour's flame
They flickered sometimes, some went out and had to be relit
It made us laugh, and that was fine
Laughter is a kind of prayer, an incense of the heart
I think it charms the one who came to light the world
The one who set a child apart
To show we should receive the truth
   with open eyes and innocence
The truth we learned that evening seemed to shine
And will do in the darkest caverns of so many other nights
Heaven will inhabit our communion of lights

HORRIBLE SONG

We hunch our shoulders to our ears like galloping gnus
Then hop around the church like excited kangaroos
We make our tummies wibble-wobble just like jellies
We dive to the floor and we wriggle on our bellies
We leap up in the air like a jack-in-the-box
Then we turn to our neighbour and we all swop socks
And are we getting weary? No!
Are we getting bored? No!
Are we feeling silly? No!
We do it for the Lord!

We do a Scottish hornpipe and we wiggle with our hips
We make a funny noise with our fingers and our lips
We croak like a frog (Ribbit!) growl like a bear (Rrrrr!)
We tap the ones in front of us and ruffle up their hair
We grab at both the shoulders of a mister or a miss
Then we all love each other with a great big sloppy kiss
And are we getting weary? No!
Are we getting bored? No!
Are we feeling silly? No!
We do it for the Lord!

We cuddle someone skinny and we dance with someone fat
We open up a Bible and we wear it like a hat
We climb up on our chairs and pretend we're chimpanzees
Then we roll our skirts and trousers up
    and feel each others' knees
And when the whole thing's over, with a chuckle and a grin
We tickle all the grumpy ones who've not been joining in
And are we getting weary? No!
Are we getting bored? No!
Are we feeling silly? No!
We do it for the Lord!

ONCE I WALKED WITH YOU

Forgive me, Lord, for once I walked with you
But when I found some level ground I pitched my tent
And there I stayed, on comfort and on pleasure bent
Yet when they asked why I was settled there
I looked them in the face, and said with conscious pride,
'My Lord, my friend, my Jesus brought me to this place'
Yesterday, by means that you will know
I learned that birds in parks are tamed by being fed
So saddened was I by this dreadful truth
That when I went to bed I cried and could not rest nor sleep
But look the dawn has come
There is no time, no cause to worry or to weep
I see you in the distance still
And as you walk you turn your head and smile
I only wish to follow you, and I shall try to be content
If I am never more allowed a place to lay my head,
Or any pleasant level ground
    on which to pitch my foolish tent.

WHEN IN DOUBT

Though Moses, Micah, Obadiah
Habakkuk and Ruth
Teach us how to live our lives
In wisdom and in truth,
There is one voice whose clear command
You must obey or rue it,
The mighty prophet Nike teaches,
'When in doubt – Just *do* it!'

1985-1990

Hall of mirrors: *Clearing away the rubbish*
When I was a small boy: *Join the company*
Growbag world: *Clearing away the rubbish*
Gatwick airport: *Clearing away the rubbish*
Shell: *Clearing away the rubbish*
The preacher: *Clearing away the rubbish*
Stress: *Clearing away the rubbish*
Away in a gutter: *Clearing away the rubbish*
A father knows no sadness: *Clearing away the rubbish*
The dream of being special: *Clearing away the rubbish*
Poison pools: *Join the company*
When does the joy start: *Clearing away the rubbish*
I didn't have to see you: *Join the company*
Winter walk: *Join the Company*
Shades of blue: *Clearing away the rubbish*
I watch: *Clearing away the rubbish*
When I became a Christian: *Clearing away the rubbish*
Hallelujah in the back of my mind : *Clearing away the rubbish*
The real problem: *Clearing away the rubbish*
Why did he choose?: *Clearing away the rubbish*
Daffodils: *Join the company*
Nathan rap: *Clearing away the rubbish*
I want to be with you: *Clearing away the rubbish*

1990–1995

Ministry: *View from a bouncy castle*
Cricket: *View from a bouncy castle*
Creed: *Cabbages for the King*
Diet: *Cabbages for the King*
Failure: *The unlocking*
Poor sad child: *Alien at St Wilfrid's*
New to me: *Cabbages for the King*
Arts group: *View from a bouncy castle*
When I was small: *The unlocking*
Jenny: *Cabbages for the King*
Angel: *Alien at St Wilfrid's*
Anglican Rap: *Cabbages for the King*
Sacred heart: *You say tomato*
I mothered she: *View from a bouncy castle*
Am I the only one: *Cabbages for the King*
Bibles and rifles: *The unlocking*
Dear family: *Cabbages for the King*
Graces: *Cabbages for the King*
Getting there: *The unlocking*
Hills of home: *The unlocking*
Landing: *The unlocking*
Worry: *Cabbages for the King*
Generations: *Cabbages for the King*
Christmas: *Cabbages for the King*
Heaven: *The unlocking*
Death: *Alien at St Wilfrid's*

1995–2000

Learning to fly: *Learning to fly*
Wild affairs: *Learning to fly*
Jacqueline: *Learning to fly*
Anglican Alphabet: *A Year at St Yorick's*
Forgive us if we say: *When you walk*
Grown-ups: *Learning to fly*
United in glory: *Father to the man*
Autumn: *When you walk*
Death of a traffic warden: *When You walk*
Soweto 1993: *Learning to fly*
Andromeda Veal to the Pope: *Horizontal epistles of Andromeda Veal*
Winchester cathedral: *Learning to fly*
Too much dying: *Learning to fly*
I want to be touched: *When you walk*
Freely I confess: *The sacred diary of Adrian Plass, Christian speaker, aged 45¾*
Night talk: *When you walk*
Cosier than cottages: *Learning to fly*
Confessing: *Learning to fly*

2000-2005

With the rest: *Why I follow Jesus*
What of me?: *Never mind the reversing ducks*
Crazy golf: *Why I follow Jesus*
To be a pilgrim: *Never mind the reversing ducks*
Winter waking: *Why I follow Jesus*
When you slept: *Never mind the reversing ducks*
Poverty: *Colours of survival*
Bangladeshi baby: *Colours of survival*
Image of the invisible God: *Never mind the reversing ducks*
No agenda: *unpublished*
Statistics of death: *Never mind the reversing ducks*
And Jesus will be born: *And Jesus will be born*

2005-2010

If I was God I wouldn't let the children die:
   Fountains in the dust
A little girl picks up a stick by High Force waterfall:
   Seriously funny
Someone I knew: *Seriously funny*
What is God?: *unpublished*
Lewis and friends: *unpublished*
Days of my life: *Bacon sandwiches and salvation*
Holes in your life: *Bacon sandwiches and salvation*
Elbows and ephods: *Bacon sandwiches and salvation*
Damn! I wish I'd prayed: *Bacon sandwiches and salvation*
Sister: The battle for Darky Green: *unpublished in UK*
Hungry rich men: *unpublished*
The head came in by helicopter: *Fountains in the dust*
Communion of lights: *Fountains in the dust*
Horrible song: *Looking good, being bad*
Once I walked with you: *unpublished*
When in doubt: *unpublished*

INDEX OF FIRST LINES

1990–1995

1995–2000

2000–2005

2005–2010

PUBLISHERS AND PUBLICATION DATES OF ORIGINAL WORKS:

Harper Collins – now Zondervan

Join the company, 1986

Clearing away the rubbish, 1988

Horizontal Epistles of Andromeda Veal, 1998

View from a bouncy castle, 1991

Alien at St Wilfreds, 1992

Cabbages for the King, 1993

You say tomato, 1995

The sacred diary of Adrian Plass, Christian speaker Aged 45¾, 1996

Father to the man, 1997

A Year at St Yoricks, 1998

Colours of survival, 2000

Why I follow Jesus, 2000

And Jesus will be born, 2003

Never mind the reversing ducks, 2002

BRF

The unlocking, 1994

When you walk, 1997

Paternoster Publishing

Learning to fly, 1996

Solway

Words from the cross, 1998

Authentic

Bacon sandwiches and salvation, 2007

Fountains in the dust, 2008

Looking good being bad, 2009

Seriously funny, 2010 (with Jeff Lucas)